Colony, Cult and Culture

Colony, Cult and Culture
Alfredo Bosi

Edited by
Pedro Meira Monteiro

Translated by
Robert P. Newcomb

University of Massachusetts Dartmouth
Dartmouth, Massachusetts

Luso-Asio-Afro-Brazilian Studies & Theory 1

Editor
Victor K. Mendes, University of Massachusetts Dartmouth

Editorial Board
Hans Ulrich Gumbrecht, Stanford University
Anna M. Klobucka, University of Massachusetts Dartmouth
João Cezar de Castro Rocha, University of Manchester
Phillip Rothwell, Rutgers University, New Brunswick
Miguel Tamen, Universidade de Lisboa

Manuscript Editor
Anna M. Klobucka

Cover Design
Inês Sena

We are thankful to Maureen Bisilliat for the permission to use the cover image, which comes from her photographic essay inspired by the work of João Guimarães Rosa.

Library of Congress Cataloging-in-Publication Data
Bosi, Alfredo, 1936-
[Dialética da colonização. Colônia, culto e cultura English.]
Colony, cult and culture / Alfredo Bosi ; edited by Pedro Meira Monteiro; translated by Robert P. Newcomb.
    p. cm.
Includes bibliographical references and index.
ISBN 978-0-9814580-0-7
1. Brazil--Civilization. 2. Brazil--History--Philosophy. 3. Brazil--Colonization. 4. Literature and history--Brazil. I. Monteiro, Pedro Meira. II. Title.
F2510.B6713 2008
981'.03072--dc22   2008002793

Table of Contents

Preface
The Dialectic of Resistance: Alfredo Bosi, Literary Critic

Pedro Meira Monteiro

Born in São Paulo in 1936, Alfredo Bosi is one of the most notable intellectuals from a generation that, arriving on the scene and establishing itself during the second half of the twentieth century, is responsible for the great critical paradigms that continue to guide academic production in Brazil. If we may situate Bosi alongside Antonio Candido and Roberto Schwarz, names that are better known to an English-speaking public, this is because, despite their differences and singularities, there is something that unites them at a deeper level: they each seek, in their own way, to understand the phenomena of a literature and a culture whose production is grounded in a peripheral experience—in this case, Brazilian—that develops in the seductive shadow of models originating in the North, especially in Europe, and always in consonance or conflict with these models. More broadly, we might imagine that the valorization of a culture produced in the molds of a peripheral formation is an essential part of a debate that applies to all of Latin America. Or, thinking of the fissures in a totalizing national discourse, we might be close to what can be identified, using a terminology more palatable to the Anglo-American academic sensibility, as a properly *liminal* culture—a term at least as old as Victor Turner's writings and employed here with the meaning that Homi Bhabha ascribes to it.[1]

Though Bosi's text was born under the sign of a critical constellation somewhat removed from contemporary theoretical debates in North America and Great Britain, it shares with them an astonishment before the complexity and richness of a world constructed against the tide of hegemonic discourses and that ultimately establishes itself in a symbolic space crisscrossed by the violent forces of colonization or, more recently, littered with the ruins of colonial power. Here a plane of conflicts and contradictions is drawn, a plane where all of the "ghosts" of the "repressed" will appear—to cite a metaphor recent studies have borrowed from the language of psychoanalysis in order to understand how forces that surge forth from the margins regularly put in check the wholeness of a national discourse with pretensions to inclusiveness. That which is repressed and then (re)appears in phantasmagoric form in the contemporary cultural and political scene ultimately designates the "performative time" of a site of resistance comprised of the *people* themselves. Bhabha looks to Fanon in seeking to comprehend that "zone of occult instability where the people dwell," which from a postcolonial (and, to be exact, postmodern) perspective points to the ephemeral temporality of all discourses (Bhabha 303). It is here, I believe, that both the meeting point and the point of divergence with respect to Bosi's analysis of culture are to be found. After all, the performative space of the popular is for the Brazilian writer less ephemeral in nature than it would appear from Bhabha's perspective. Where contemporary theory, produced by a largely Anglophone academy, might see the imminent dissolution of all identities, Bosi's contemporaneous reflections seek out the daily re-composition of something that, while not constituting a fixed or stable identity, establishes itself as a strong environment for the reaffirmation of the repressed—a "repressed" that in both theoretical visions invokes memory, ritual, and myth in composing the performative space of its own resistance. In this book, this is referred to as the "dialectic of colonization."

Before briefly reflecting in this Preface on the meaning of the critical project proposed and announced by Bosi's essay, it would be useful to inform the reader of the partial character of "Colônia, culto e cultura" (Colony, Cult and Culture): published in 1992, it is the opening chapter of a long book entitled *Dialética da colonização* (Dialectic of Colonization), which has been reprinted many times in Brazil and translated in its entirety into French and Spanish. The book contains ten essays on Brazilian literature as well as addenda that reconsider the critical material or specify the conditions and context of the text's production, along with an epilogue that accompanies more recent versions of the text, beginning with the 2001 edition.[2]

The book that the reader has in hand is the product of a dual effort aimed first at making a seminal essay from the Brazilian critical imagination accessible to an English-language reading public, and second, at placing Alfredo Bosi's name in the space that is rightfully his, among the great critical voices of Latin America that are present in the complex environment of reflection on culture in English.

***

Alfredo Bosi tells us in his 1992 "Acknowledgements" that *Dialética da colonização* began with the courses on Brazilian literature he taught at the University of São Paulo in the 1970s. Here he perhaps inadvertently provides us with a first, decisive clue for understanding his critical project: the material Bosi brought together was weighed down by the spirit of a particular age. As a critical intervention and theoretical reference point, *Dialética da colonização* was born under one more brutal Latin American dictatorship, which both reawakened the ghosts of domination and fear and brought critics and writers to join the ranks of a multiform resistance that was not always completely organized or coherent.3 Literature's referential power, which allows it to speak of what is generally silenced, is especially important in such historical periods. In this sense, one would be justified in imagining Alfredo Bosi in his *Dialética da colonização* pondering, by way of a masterful analysis of a literary garment sewn together over various periods, the existence of forces that resist power's instantiations and machinations and that oppose, to the brutal mug of violence, the ambiguous and quite often liberating face of the letter.

The idea of resistance appears throughout Bosi's oeuvre. In a classic essay published also during the decade of the 1970s, "Poesia resistência" (Poetry resistance), Bosi described a "mytho-poetic will" already under threat from the "mechanisms of interest, of productivity," with it ultimately falling to poetry to gather "those residual elements of the landscape, of memory and of dreams that the culture industry has not yet succeeded in manipulating for sale" (142).

The terminology used reflects the era in which the essay was written (with a word's *time* being itself a theme of absolute importance to Bosi), and reveals a deep desire to view poetic production as a possible instance

9

of resistance. The "dialectic" that announced itself in Bosi's writing from the 1970s is less a teleological movement of consciousness capable of categorically revealing history's future course than it is the power to, in the context of a daily existence emptied of meaning, scrape at a wound where a certain liberating potential still shows forth. From this time forward a muted, insistent battle is fought, whose sounds of conflict resound in Bosi's texts. This is a battle against the "haughty autism" of words that represent themselves, that are subdued in the metalinguistic exercises of modern (or postmodern) poetry, and that are always ready to lose their original link with what we might dare to call *community*—a community of meanings and of peoples in which subjects share their experience with others and reencounter and discover themselves in the presence of those who are like them. The subject does this through the liberating power of language, by rediscovering the "living meaning" of poetic language among the silence that this language, being at the same time sound and poetry, delicately guards. Still in the 1970s, Bosi echoed Hegel in suggesting that though they were always close to each other, the poetic word and music differ because in the case of poetry the word, from an "end in itself," is turned into "a means of spiritual expression." He adds: "It is true that verbal expression loses 'the independence and the freedom of sounds' that is peculiar to music; but the silence that appears after the final word guards, in the folds of perception of the person who hears it, the speaker's way of being. The tone, prolonged in the pause, has an interpersonal reach" (Bosi, *O ser e o tempo* 106). It is not difficult to detect in the phrase's Hegelian impulse echoes of an even deeper belief that informs Bosi's critical militancy, which is the "at once simple and profound sight" hidden in Croce's definition of poetry as "a complex of images and the feeling that animates them" (Bosi, "Sobre alguns modos" 8).

In a certain sense, this "feeling" that animates literary material points to a *subject* that we customarily think of, from a modern or postmodern perspective, as divided, ripped apart, or simply fragmentary. In order to accurately understand Bosi's critical project, however, one must not suppose that what guides it is a simple nostalgia for a whole and unpolluted subject that is said to be lost in contemporary experience. On the contrary, Bosi always refers to a divided subject that is wounded at its core. At the same time, he is never interested in the simple chronicling of subjective fragmentation: what interests him is the seeking out in texts of that *animus* that sustains them as intersubjective provocations, the search for what meaning remains in them. And here I cannot fail to note that for Saint Augustine to *signify* meant precisely the capacity to make signals (*signa facere*), to produce something that the subject knows and in which he recognizes himself, since language itself can be a singular and irreproducible experience for the subjects and their interlocutors.

Alfredo Bosi's critical vocabulary, a highly complex mixture of theoretical and philosophical references, resounds of time, or rather it resounds *in time*: it is a lofty, risky bet on the value of human experience that would become lost in the market, and that capitalism would transform, without compassion or pity, into merchandise. But terms and concepts used in literary analysis are not and cannot be exact copies of the vocabulary belonging to the epoch in which the critic is situated. The spirit that animates a particular analysis may flow, and indeed flows, from the needs and concerns of the present. However, the study of literary material requires a dialog that applies synchronically and diachronically to the letter of the text being analyzed. The challenge becomes one of understanding the horizon of possibilities the writer finds open to him or her at the time of writing. Let Father Vieira serve as an example: it is not by chance that Bosi, in one of the essays that comprise *Dialética da colonização,* understands Vieira as a tortured author, deeply divided between the extremes of a "universalist discourse," which would move him to a commitment to free the slaves, and the "barrier against the universalization of man" that the "colonial condition" erected, and that caused Vieira, the defender of the Amerindians, to simultaneously make an apology for black slavery (Bosi, *Dialética* 119-48).

It is not by chance that this is the *punctum dolens* of a long-standing critical polemic, which I invoke here merely to illustrate how Bosi's criticism feeds on this mixture of hope and belief in literature's power of resistance. Many of the harshest critics of Bosi's work hold this to be an undesirable ingredient in the context of literary interpretation, since according to them an analysis that remains faithful to the mentality and the rhetorical web informing the writing of someone like Vieira should be fundamentally concerned with the author's commitment to the "practical" reasons of the Empire and his coherently counter-reformist mindset. In this mode of criticism, it would be anachronistic to speak of a divided Vieira, tortured by his own conscience.

But this is precisely the power of Alfredo Bosi's criticism, which is sure to reveal itself to the reader of *Colony, Cult and Culture*: the providentialism, the millenarianism and the utopianism that may hide within texts produced on colonial soil are often profound manifestations of a great, inherent contradiction in what the poet Gregório de Matos called the colony's *máquina mercante* (trading machine), which is maximally exploitative while simultaneously creating the space for its own superseding. To cite Ferreira Gullar's aporia, which serves as the epigraph to this book, "for us the new represents, contradictorily, liberty and submission." As we will see, to produce culture is also to venerate the dead, to remember them, and to find in the vestiges of the past the rationale and fuel for resisting the economic machine that consumes everything and everyone. In this vision of culture, literary material simultaneously belongs and does not belong to its time. Or, to put it differently, from within the rhetorical web that binds literary material to its own time this same material opens itself to other time periods that are contained in the time of writing. This is not an anachronism, but the need to perceive, or dare to imagine, that there is always a subject, a contradictory figure by definition, hiding behind the text. This subject speaks not only within his or her own time, precisely because he or she also speaks to us, the inhabitants of another time.

I assume that in reading this book the reader will feel the spirit of the time revealing itself, as an illumination, in certain passages. The hopes that individuals have invented always and throughout the ages to withstand pain and suffering march in succession before our eyes. The text is also music, and the attentive reader will hear echoes of many of the appeals for resistance voiced during our own time: from the critique of consumer society to a veiled hope for a return to community; from the alternative society so intensely rehearsed by the counterculture to contemporary Third-World theories of underdevelopment. All this suggests that there lies concealed in *Colony, Cult and Culture* a theoretical corpus that ranges from Marxist-oriented sociological criticism to the humanism of Liberation Theology, all mediated by a perplexity before the sometimes liberating, sometimes imprisoning power of language.

Words of resistance, taken from the roots of resistance: this is what Alfredo Bosi's criticism can offer when it dives into the depths of a text, a space where the spirit finds a relief that is nothing more than the inverted, magnificent sign of its own misery.

***

Colony, Cult and Culture cannot be reduced to strict referentiality. I do not think that in a text like this one should only look for "information" on the Brazilian "case." The reader will of course find references to the history of the Portuguese colony in America, and will become especially aware of how Alfredo Bosi positions himself in relation to the Brazilian critical and historiographical traditions, recognizing their merits and observing their limitations. This said, Bosi's reflection here is broader in scope: it seeks to understand the production of literature (or of what has been produced "beyond the pale of writing") in its capacity as a fundamental, dialectical element of resistance to an overwhelming, conformity-enforcing power that, in the colonial context, advances unabashedly and often without any constraint. Ultimately, the colony is the space in which the trajectories along which commercial capital advances (with industrial capital following in its wake) are revealed in their full force. And yet it is this same space, crisscrossed by violence and ironically described by Marx as "idyllic," that produces forms of resistance, which, archaizing as they are, can paradoxically speak to modern consciousness in loud voices. From the depths of a land that capital tends to destroy, a dissonant and beautiful voice surges forth. Bosi will seek out this voice alternately in an erudite register that formalizes and sublimates popular experience, and in an oral register that deforms cultured themes in order to press them into the service of people's experience, which is always full of meaning.

The collection of cultured authors brought together for Bosi's profound analysis of resistance in the colonial context is a large one: there are the Jesuits from the first phase of colonization in the sixteenth century, the satirical poet Gregório de Matos and Father Vieira from the seventeenth, Basílio da Gama and the Neoclassical *árcades* poets of Minas Gerais from the eighteenth, the epic and lyric Renaissance poet Luís de Camões, the modernist Anglophone poet T.S. Eliot, the chroniclers of the Portuguese colony, the travelers, the great theorists: Marx, Burckhardt, Gilberto Freyre, Sérgio Buarque de Holanda, Celso Furtado. And then there are other artists and figures, even more fundamentally at home in the matter the critic seeks out in his avenging desire to understand resistance in the complexity of its forms. These are located on the border between the popular and the erudite, and the colonial-era Baroque-popular sculptor

Aleijadinho is chief among them. Additionally, and as the reader will see, the literary critic attentively and emotionally recounts the performance of a religious hymn he witnessed on the outskirts of São Paulo. To his (and our) amazement, the hymn combines erudite medieval poetry with the popular, provincial and entirely un-modern "caipira" tone of the singers and those leading the ceremony, and compels us to consider the complex weave of meanings contained in the idea of culture. "Cult" and "culture" are precisely the initial terms of Bosi's text, and are the words by the way of which the book's reader is invited to penetrate the hidden caverns of the complex historical process that is colonization, with all of its marks, wounds, advances, and retreats.

An additional word on a central aspect of this book: since "culture" is its principal object of study, and as Bosi seeks to comprehend it in the context of the Luso-Brazilian colonial and postcolonial formation, the problem of acculturation logically occupies a central space in his analysis, particularly in terms of the notion of a "mixed" tradition and production in which not only the "high" and "low" registers mix, but in which the idea of the "reinterpretation" of one culture by another (this is a term Bosi takes from Herskovits) takes on an absolute and constant importance. The complex themes of *hybridization* and *miscegenation,* so appealing to our contemporary academic curiosity, both within and outside of Brazil, are foundational elements of Bosi's analysis. The reader will see how, in this book, a severe though respectful critique of theoretical models taken from Sérgio Buarque de Holanda's and Gilberto Freyre's classic analyses is coupled with a timely discussion of the sublimation of violence in discourses on race relations. This sublimation leads, or may lead, to the idealization of Brazil as a country that, less affected by a rigid segregationist logic of the type established in the United States, would have achieved the mysterious and long-desired ideal of a racial democracy. It is precisely on the often unseen (or concealed) aspect of violence that Bosi focuses when he analyses miscegenation in all its diversity and depth.

A final observation on the *words* that Bosi so skillfully works in his essay and that carry much of the weight of his reflection on culture and its forms. At a certain point, he makes the important distinction between the colonial "system" and the colonial "condition." The colonial "system" can be measured and analyzed, and provides the basis for an economy organized by a colonial logic, oriented toward agricultural exportation and monoculture, and based on forced labor and the greatest possible exploitation of the environment and the people. The colonial "condition" refers to "a more diffuse set of experiences" on the part of historical subjects, who cannot simply be reduced to the role attributed to them by the economic system, but who in the very heart of this system discover the fissures and wounds where they will shelter the dreams, hopes, sufferings, and doubts they have as people of flesh and bone. It is in the *colonial condition*, within the overarching *colonial system,* that an alert Bosi will seek out the voice of his subjects—a voice we could ultimately term the *vox populi*. This is an extremely important element, which allows the reader to identify this book as part of a long tradition of reflection on popular culture.

It would not be amiss, perhaps, to look for the roots of Bosi's concern with the *popular* in an intellectual tradition that goes at least as far back as the attention paid by Brazilian modernism to themes and elements belonging to the "people," among them their speech and songs. In absorbing and reacting to many of the ideas championed by the European vanguards at the beginning of the twentieth century, Brazilian modernism encompassed all those artists who, seeking to poetically recover the "people" without falling into the trap of Romantic idealization and stylization, programmatically incorporated the popular—its ways of speaking and feeling—into the realms of literature, music and the plastic arts. The person who went farthest in this mission, or dream, may have been the poet and fiction writer Mário de Andrade (1893-1945), who in his time was also a dedicated folklorist. At the same time, Bosi's search for the "popular" has little to do with the folklorist's cataloguing effort, and is much closer to those moments that in English-language academic writings on popular culture are termed "moments of freedom," and which Juan Flores recently borrowed from the title of a book by Johannes Fabian.

Nevertheless, there are differences in tone: placing Bosi in the context of contemporary criticism dealing with popular culture it is possible to argue that he reacts with a certain skepticism to the dominion of "mass culture," as if "archaizing" content were essential for the constitution of those moments that, as this book will show, lead to the momentary affirmation of *another* identity, radically resistant to the sterilized identities that the "system" creates and recreates on the symbolic plane. It is from the colonial, or postcolonial, "condition" that truly epiphanic moments are born, moments of affirmation of an Other who resists, let it be said once

15

more, the economic machinery of the "system." But from Bosi's perspective resistance is only possible through the selective exercise of memory. And here the Brazilian critic again approximates Juan Flores's discussion of the "pueblo pueblo." In the end, the possibility of capturing those "moments of freedom" is only opened to those who perceive the "arts of timing" and substitute a more nuanced vision for a merely spatial conception of the "popular," noting that ultimately the location of the "popular" is temporal and historical rather than geographic.

Therefore, what the cultural critic looks for, or should look for, are those spaces in which dominated subjects overlay diverse temporalities and force them to dialog with one another, constructing an environment in which the freedom of the people is revealed, albeit fleetingly. This is a momentary freedom that is the more moving and meaningful for being transitory and unrepeatable.

Princeton, NJ, November 2007

Notes

[1] "What might be the cultural and political effects of the liminality of the nation, the margins of modernity, which cannot be signified without the narrative temporalities of splitting, ambivalence, and vacillation?" (Bhabha 298).

[2] In addition to its opening essay, which is published here for the first time in English, *Dialética da colonização* contains chapters on the sixteenth-century Jesuit José de Anchieta ("Anchieta ou as flechas opostas do sagrado"), seventeenth-century satirical poet Gregório de Matos ("Do antigo Estado à máquina mercante"), Father Vieira ("Vieira ou a cruz da desigualdade"), Vieira's fellow Jesuit and chronicler of the seventeenth-century sugar plantation João Antonio Andreoni, or Antonil ("Antonil ou as lágrimas da mercadoria"), nineteenth-century novelist and politician José de Alencar ("Um mito sacrificial: o indianismo de Alencar"), on the strange coupling of a slave-holding mentality and liberal consciousness in nineteenth-century Brazil ("A escravidão entre dois liberalismos"), on the awareness of slavery's horrors, before and after the 1888 abolition, in authors like Castro Alves, Lima Barreto and Cruz e Sousa ("Sob o signo de Cam"), on the positivist roots of the idea of a centralizing welfare state in Brazil ("A arqueologia do Estado-providên-

cia"), on a typology of contemporary cultural production, understood through a balancing of the erudite and the popular ("Cultura brasileira e culturas brasileiras"), and finally, a synthesis of the results of the author's research ("Olhar em retrospecto").

3 The Brazilian dictatorship, inscribed in the cycle of Cold War-era Latin American dictatorships supported by the government of the United States, lasted from 1964 to 1985, when a civilian politician who emerged from the authoritarian government's traditional support base was elevated to the presidency of the country. The first direct elections for the Brazilian presidency to follow the dictatorship took place in 1989.

Author's Note for the North-American Edition

Alfredo Bosi

In writing "Colony, Cult and Culture" as an introduction to *Dialética da colonização,* the challenge I faced consisted in creating a space of convergence that would bring together some of the conceptual planes that are fundamental to the process of colonization. In this search for a common denominator capable of including the diversity of historical elements involved in this process without reducing them to the unity of an abstract term, I was aided by the very etymology of the words *colony* and *colonization.*

As the reader will perceive in the opening pages of the essay, both words have as their root the Latin verb *colo,* from which the terms *colony, cult* and *culture* all derive. These are not mere lexical coincidences, but actual historical dimensions that interact with one another throughout the colonial period, and which may be recognized even today in postcolonial societies. The general idea that underlies these three dimensions is that of labor—physical, moral and intellectual.

The colonizer is he who takes control of a foreign land and by means of force, technique, and skill, conquers it, exploits it, cultivates it, and dominates it politically; in sum, he exercises all the powers brought together in the verb *colo,* whose deverbal noun form is *colony.* In the interest of an accurate understanding of this process, economics and other social sciences may be called upon to research the material conditions that governed colonization. This assignment has already been successfully accomplished by some of our best historians, among them Capistrano de Abreu, Caio Prado Jr., Celso Furtado, Raymundo Faoro, and Jacob Gorender. I used their work in my own as an indispensable reference for any study of our economic and political formation.

There is, of course, no colonizing agent without a past or without memory. Conquerors did not spring forth from an atemporal zero-degree point. They brought with them in their caravels beliefs that conditioned their attitudes toward the native populations they came to dominate, when they did not destroy them altogether. Together with the sword and the blunderbuss came the cross and the Bible. The Iberian, English and French colonies were populated by men who practiced either a popular and still medieval Catholicism or its counter-reformist version, or a puritanical Protestantism in revolt against Anglican hegemony. Monotheism brought them together as Christians opposed to "indigenous paganism," though they were divided into active or passive contemporaries of the Inquisition, the Reformation, or the Counter-Reformation, and by the religious wars fought during the sixteenth and seventeenth centuries. How can one understand José de Anchieta's Latin and Tupi plays or the sermons of Father Antônio Vieira (both missionaries and Jesuit writers whom I studied in individual chapters of *Dialética da colonização*) without examining in depth the peculiar quality of the Medieval and later Baroque Catholic *cult?* How can one arbitrarily separate the missionary spirit from the project of colonization? How is it possible to separate colony-as-cultivation from colony-as-cult? How can their spaces of convergence and divergence be detected?

A parallel question may be directed to scholars of Anglo-Saxon colonization in the United States: how can this process be understood without exploring the religious and moral lives of the Puritans established there in the seventeenth and eighteenth centuries? In the Old as in the New World, and particularly during this period—prior to the Industrial Revolution and full-blown bourgeois hegemony—the relations between the economic structure and religious ideas and practices were so interconnected that they can only be entirely separated in the context of specialized (and, in truth, one-sided) academic studies.

The third dimension of the colonization process entails the development of a secular culture, heralded from the Renaissance forward and polemically advanced beginning in the Enlightenment. The word *culture* derives from the future participle of the verb *colo* and points toward the notion of a project: what must be cultivated, what must be built; that is, a set of virtual ideas and values that are a given in the minds and the wills of a certain social and intellectual group. This dimension became a fundamental component of the process of independence led by the New World's propertied classes and lettered elites, component that shaped the model of political rupture with the colonizing metropolis. Liberal European culture was the ideological cement binding together the emancipatory battles that broke out in all of Latin America during the first quarter of the nineteenth century. Later, with the Republic proclaimed, positivist principles would inspire a politics of *order and progress,* which the leaders of the Revolution of 1930 in Brazil went on to translate into the forms of centralized government and state-led industrialization.

***

As the historian takes into consideration the multiple expressions of a given period's symbolic universe, his attention is drawn to the existence of diverging and, when taken to the limit, contradictory tendencies of thought and of *pathos.* The conventional historicism that dominated the literary histories of the nineteenth century transformed those authors and works that departed from their period's standard style into exceptions or singular manifestations of backwardness or deviation (the *attardés* and *égarés* discussed by Gustave Lanson in his important history of French literature); in the best of cases, it celebrated the anticipatory qualities of some *precursors.*

In contrast to pure historicism, the dialectical vision of culture, adopting a Hegelian-Marxian approach, recognizes in the coexisting contradictions of every worldview the very dynamic of a history made up of tensions between dominant ideologies and the forces of resistance. Or, in Hegelian terms, it detects the tensions between the affirmative thrust of the thesis and the negative force of the antithesis. As long as this method is not automatized into a facile game of affirmations, negations and sublations, it can offer a fruitful way for dealing with diversity and the conflicts inherent to each social formation in each of its historical moments. This is the most general meaning of the term "dialectic," as featured in the title of the book whose introduction the English-language reader now has in hand.

In the chapter "Olhar em retrospecto" (A Retrospective Glance), which closes *Dialética da colonização,* I synthesized the results of my research and my reflections on the book's object of study in these terms:

"Colonization is a process that is at once material and symbolic. The economic practices of its agents are linked to their means of survival, to their memory, to their ways of representing themselves and others, and ultimately, to their desires and hopes. To put it another way: there is no colonial condition without a weaving together of cults, of ideologies and of cultures. The relations between these fundamental dimensions (which Marxism summarized at the levels of infra- and superstructure) are modified, throughout time, by positive determinants of adjustment, reproduction and continuity. Situations arise, however, in which it is the asymmetries and, in extreme cases, the ruptures that appear before the historian and anthropologist of colonial life." The dialectical approach teaches us that we should pay just as much attention to moments of tension and change as to states of equilibrium and adjustment. Diachrony is only possible because synchrony is neither homogeneous nor static.

***

The corpus from which the examples considered in my book were taken belongs entirely to the history of Brazilian culture and, in several cases, to the history of the ideologies, counter-ideologies, and utopias constituted throughout the colonial and postcolonial periods. Insofar as each one of these complexes of symbols and values *was of interest* to the social groups that participated in the historical drama (here I draw on the strong meaning given by Habermas to the term *interest*), and given the extent to which respective ideologies and counter-ideologies played an effective role in this same drama, one may affirm that *superstructural phenomena always occupy a place in the history of a people*. It is the understanding of this place that draws the eye of the scholar of colonization.

I hope that my discussion is sufficiently clear, as well as instructive whenever possible, so that the text that follows may be understood by readers who are unfamiliar with Brazilian cultural and literary history. I am grateful to Robert Patrick Newcomb, the translator of this essay, who took on the sometimes difficult task of composing in English what I attempted to say in Portuguese. To Victor K. Mendes, who thought it opportune to make my text available to scholars interested in Brazil, and to Pedro Meira Monteiro, whose intellectual generosity was responsible for this edition, my heartfelt thanks.

Institute for Advanced Studies, University of São Paulo
December 2007

Colony, Cult and Culture

For

Celso Furtado
Jacob Gorender
Pedro Casaldáliga

thought made action

O novo é para nós, contraditoriamente, a liberdade e a submissão.

[For us the new represents, contradictorily, liberty and submission.]

Ferreira Gullar

I. Colo-Cultus-Cultura

It may not be in vain to begin with words. Relationships between phenomena leave marks on the body of language. The words *culture, cult* and
colonization all derive from the Latin verb *colo*, whose past participle is
cultus and whose future participle is *culturus*.

In the language of Rome, *colo* signified *I live on, I occupy the land*, and
by extension, *I work on and cultivate the land*.[i] *Incola*, or inhabitant, is an
early descendent of *colo*. *Inquilinus*, one who resides in a foreign land, is
another. *Agricola* belongs to a second semantic plane linked to the idea of
work.

In the present tense, *colo* implies something incomplete or transitive, a
movement that passes, or has been passing, from agent to object. *Colo* is
the root of *colonia* as a space in the process of being occupied, a land and
people that can be worked on and subjected. For his part, "*Colonus* is he
who cultivates a rural landholding in place of the owner, its administrator
in the technical and legal sense of the word. This is found in Plautus and
Cato as *colonia* [...]; the colony's inhabitant, in Greek the *ápoikos*, who
establishes himself in the place of the *incolae* (Magne).[ii]

It is not coincidental that whenever the various types of colonization
are distinguished, so are two processes: that which attains to the populat-
ing of the colony and that which refers to the cultivation of the land. The
idea of *colo* is present in both: I live in, I cultivate.

The Roman legal code is present in the verbal expression attached to
the act of colonizing. What, then, distinguishes habitation and cultivation
from colonization? In principle, it is the social agents' transplanting of
their world onto another, where they will work the foreign land or have
others do this for them. The *incola* who emigrates becomes a *colonus*.

Mechanisms of production and relations of power, the economic and
political spheres, are reproduced and reinforced—as if they were true uni-
versals of human societies—whenever a cycle of colonization begins.

But colonization is not limited to the re-articulation of these basic features: there is the structural *plus* of domination, an added concentration of forces around the figure of the conqueror that bestows on him, at times, epic connotations of risk and adventure. Colonization gives established cultures an air of rebirth and advancement.

The marked presence of domination is inherent to colonization in its various forms and almost always overdetermines them. *To take care of,* the basic meaning of *colo,* not only implies *attentiveness,* but also *ordering.* It is true that the colonist does not always see himself exclusively as a conqueror; he will try to imprint on the minds of his descendents the image of a discoverer and settler, titles that legitimate him as a pioneer. In 1556, by which time the *leyenda negra* (black legend) of Spanish colonization was already spreading over Christian Europe, the use of the words *conquista* (conquest) and *conquistadores* (conquerors) was officially prohibited in Spain, and they were substituted by *descubrimiento* (discovery) and *pobladores* (settlers)—that is, colonists.[1]

During antiquity, the rise of powerful political structures corresponded to the establishment of true imperial systems that followed wars of conquest. The Middle Eastern empires of Alexander and the Romans are among the oldest known concentrations of state power. In the case of Rome, the central organization of the state resisted disintegration until the barbarian invasions atomized Europe, opening the way for the continent's eventual feudalization.

Multiple hypotheses purport to explain the genesis of these systems. The internal tensions that occur in a given social formation resolve themselves, whenever possible, in outward-looking movements of desire, search for, and conquest of, lands and peoples capable of being colonized. In this way, demographic imbalance may have been one of the causes of the ancient Greeks' colonization of the Mediterranean between the eighth and sixth centuries B.C. Likewise, Portugal's growing need for foreign commercial markets during the strenuous rise of the bourgeoisie served as an important factor in the kingdom's fifteenth-century expansion.[iii] In neither case can colonization be treated as a simple migratory movement: instead, it represents the resolution of conflicts and the meeting of needs, as well as an attempt to reassert, under new conditions, one's dominion over nature and other people—an effort that invariably accompanies the so-called civilizing process.

In passing, at this point, from the present tense of *colo,* with all its connotations of immediate activity and power, to the nominal forms of the
verb, *cultus* and *cultura,* I must leave the here-and-now for the mediated
realms of the past and future.

The past: as a deverbal adjective, *cultus* refers to the land that successive generations have cleared and planted. *Cultus* connotes not only the
perpetually repeated action conveyed by *colo,* implying cultivation over
the centuries, but, especially, the qualities that result from this labor and
that are incorporated into the worked land. When peasants from Latium
referred to their cultivated land as *culta,* they sought to convey a cumula-
tive meaning: both the act of cultivation in itself and the countless hours of
necessary labor it absorbed. This gives the participle *cultus,* a noun that is
also a verb, a more dense and vivid signifying form than is implied by the
simple naming of present labor. The Latin *ager cultus* and another deverbal, the Portuguese *roçado* (both meaning cultivated land), join the idea
of systematic work to the quality obtained from that work, an association
that becomes part of the speaker's emotional world. *Cultus* serves as a sign
that a society that produces its own food is now possessed of a memory.
The word contains the struggle between the subject and the object of collective bodily effort, and becomes a vehicle for indicating the presence of
what *was* in what occurs *now.* Process and product coexist in the same lin-
guistic sign.

As for the noun *cultus, us,* it was used to refer not only to working the
land, but also to the *cult of the dead,* a root form of religion as memory, as
the conjuring or exorcising of those who have passed from the earth.
Present-day anthropologists seem confident in their belief that sacred burial preceded the working of the soil: while the latter practice dates from the
Neolithic period and the first Agricultural Revolution (beginning around
7,000 B.C.), the dead were already being buried some 80,000 years ago,
during the time of the Neanderthals.

As Gordon Childe puts it:

> As to the magico-religious notions that held neolithic communities
> together, a few guesses may be hazarded. The tendance of the dead, going
> far back into the Old Stone Age, may have assumed a deeper significance in
> the new. In the case of several neolithic groups, indeed, no burials have
> been discovered. But generally the dead were carefully interred in built or

excavated graves, either grouped in cemeteries near the settlement or dug close to the individual dwellings. The dead are normally provided with utensils or weapons, vases of food and drink, and toilet articles. In pre-historic Egypt pictures of animals and objects are painted on the funerary vases. They presumably had the same magic significance as the cave painting and rock-carvings of Old Stone Age hunters. In historical times they were transferred to the walls of the tomb, and then attached texts show that they were really designed to ensure to the dead the continued enjoyment of the services they depict.

Such tendance denotes an attitude to the ancestral spirits that goes back to far older periods. But now the earth in which the ancestors' remains lie buried is seen as the soil from which the community's food supply magically springs each year. The ancestral spirits must surely be regarded as assisting in the crops' germination.

Fertility cults, magic rites to assist or compel the forces of reproduction, may have become more prominent than ever in neolithic times. Small figurines of women, carved in stone or ivory, with the sexual characters well marked, have been noted in camps of the Old Stone Age. But similar figures, now generally modelled in clay, are very common in neolithic settlements and graves. They are often termed "mother goddesses." Was the earth from whose womb the young grain sprouts really conceived in the likeness of a woman with whose generative functions man is certainly familiar? (101-102)[iv]

At this point it will be useful to sum up the two linked meanings of the noun-verb that shows human beings chained to the land, digging holes that nurture them while they are alive and shelter them when they are dead:

cultus (1): that which is worked *on* the land; cultivated;
cultus (2): that which is worked *in* the land; cult; burial of the dead; a ritual undertaken to honor one's ancestors.

A group's effort to root its present experience in the past is undertaken through symbolic mediation—through gestures, song, dance, ritual, prayer, verbal evocation, and verbal invocation. In the ancient world, this was all fundamentally religious and linked the present to the past-turned-present, tying a community to the forces that created it in another time and that sustain its identity.

The cult, with its continual reassertion of origins and ancestry, is another constant in human societies, along with the material struggle for survival and the relations of power that derive from it and that are implied, both literally and metaphorically, in the active form of *colo*.

In certain Greek colonies, the designs of the gods, as deciphered by the oracles, were often invoked as the causes of the settlement's foundation. In Delphi it was Apollo Archegetes who presided over the foundation of colonies. Portuguese colonizers in the Americas, in Asia and in Africa were inspired by the project of spreading the faith, just as they sought to expand the empire: "dilatando / a Fé, o Império," as Camões had it. And the Puritans who came ashore on the beaches of New England similarly declared themselves ready to perform the ways of God.

Colonization is a totalizing process whose dynamic forces can always be found at the level of *colo*: in the occupation of new land, the exploitation of its resources, and the submission of its inhabitants. But the agents of this process are not merely physical supports for the operation of eco-nomic forces; they are also believers who in the arks of memory and lan-guage carry with them their still present dead. The dead have two faces: they serve as a sword or shield in the ferocious conflicts of the everyday, but they can also make themselves heard in this theater of crime, with their pained voices conveying messages of censure and remorse. Santiago de Compostela (Saint James) rallies the *matamoros,* or moor-slayers, in the battles of the Iberian *reconquista,* and then the Cross that has defeated the Crescent is planted in the land of Brazil wood to subjugate the Tupi, but the same cross is summoned by others to preserve the freedom of the Amerindians and urge mercy for black slaves.[2] The same mass celebrated in the Jesuit missions of the Sete Povos is heard by the *bandeirantes* who, blessed by their chaplains, will mercilessly massacre the inhabitants of these settlements.[3] Did the God of the missionaries and the prophets answer to the same name as the God of the warriors and Pharisees? The key question to ask is how each group read and interpreted scripture so as to adapt religion's universalizing discourses to its particular practices.

What do religious symbols and rites, along with narratives of creation, the fall and salvation, do if not reconstruct day-to-day experience, shot through as it is with economic divisions and oppressive hierarchies of power, as an idealized totality?

31

We can derive another participle from *cultum*, the supine of *colo:* this is the future *culturus*—what will be worked, what one wishes to cultivate.

In its substantive form, the word applies to the hard work of the soil, to *agri-culture,* as well as to all the work done to a human being since infancy; in this second sense *culturus* became a Romanized form of the Greek *paideia.* Its most general meaning has been preserved to the present day, with culture understood as the sum of those practices, techniques, symbols, and values that must be transmitted to the next generation in order to guarantee the continuity of a given state of social coexistence. Education represents the institutional staging of this process.

The ending *-urus* in *culturus* communicates the idea of the future, or of forward movement. In densely urbanized societies, culture also came to be understood as a more humane form of existence, which should be strived for as the end term of a civilizing process valued more or less consciously by all social classes and groups. Culture as an ideal of personal status, by then divorced from the religious connotations of a cult, was late in coming to Rome. When it did arrive, it spread a program of *paideia* that became fixed from the fourth century B.C., as Werner Jaeger's and Henri-Irénée Marrou's important studies demonstrate. *Paideia:* an educational ideal oriented toward the formation of the adult in the *polis* and in the world.

The idea of culture presupposes a productive, laborious group consciousness that prizes out plans for the future from present circumstances. This *projective dimension,* implied in the myth of Prometheus who stole fire from the heavens in order to change the material destiny of humanity, becomes more pronounced during periods in which there are social classes or strata capable of future hopes and projects, as in the Florentine Renaissance, the eighteenth-century Enlightenment, the various scientific and technical revolutions, or during the life cycle of socialist revolutions. The modern version of Titanism, which manifests itself in theories of social evolution, extends the certainties of the Enlightenment and conceptualizes culture in opposition to nature, generating a rationalized view of history as reducible to the development (technical and otherwise) of productive forces. Culture thereby approximates the idea of *colo* as labor and distances itself, at times antagonistically, from *cultus.* The present becomes a kind of spring, an instrument in the service of the future. As culture's productive function becomes accentuated, man is obliged to gain systematic dominance over the material world and over other men. In this

COLONY, CULT AND CULTURE

context, to acculturate a people means subjecting them, or in the best of cases, adapting them technologically to a social arrangement held to be superior. In certain military-industrial regimes, this relationship is openly and unblushingly manifested. To produce is to control workers, consumers and, prospectively, citizens. Economics is politics in its brute form, and knowledge is power, to cite Francis Bacon's crude equation.

According to a certain reductive view, there is a strict connection between a society's superstructures and its economic and political sphere. It is important to recall, however, that some formative elements of modern culture (which become more apparent from the Enlightenment onward) grant science, the arts, and philosophy an inherent or virtual capacity to resist prevailing *structural* pressures. In the agonistic words of the historian Jacob Burckhardt, for whom *power is in itself evil,* the action of culture

> on the two constants [State and Church—Burckhardt was writing in the mid-nineteenth century] is one of perpetual modification and disintegration, and is limited only by the extent to which they have pressed it into their service and included it within their aims.
>
> Otherwise it is the critic of both, the clock which tells the hour at which their form and substance no longer coincide. (140)

This awareness of the capacity of culture to embody the consciousness of a present marked by sharp imbalances becomes a springboard for the creation of alternative ideas for a future that can be viewed as in some way new. Writing in another ideological context, Antonio Gramsci proposed, as prerequisites for a new cultural order, a *critique of common sense* and the *consciousness of the historicity* of one's own worldview.[v]

From the eighteenth century onward, the ideas of culture and progress have grown closer to each other, at times becoming one and the same. The fact that Enlightenment thinking was critically reflected in Hegelian-Marxian thought, in the sociology of knowledge, and in a certain phenomenology opposed to classical rationalism, did not mean that its original light was snuffed out.[vi] And, if I may venture a comparison with what occurred to Neo-Platonic idealism in its encounter with Christianity, I would say that just as Logos needed to be *made flesh* and *dwell among us* in order to reveal itself fully to humanity, so did contemporary reason seek to embody and socialize itself in its desire to transcend the dated project of the Enlightenment and protect itself from the risk of falling back on that *static philosophy of Reason* of which even Karl Mannheim himself complained, or of irresponsibly placing itself in the service of capital and the bureaucratic machine. Formerly colonized peoples have more than enough motivation and accumulated experience to distrust a manifestly neo-Enlightenment language that complacently reproduces itself in the midst of the suffering and destruction wrought by a rationalized pseudo-modernity, which has no end other than enriching itself.

However, when the light of the Enlightenment illuminates itself, and recognizes the source and the limits of its power, the contribution it makes to the human and material world carries the benefits of modestly limiting itself to saying only what it knows and promising nothing beyond what it can grant. The *dialectic of Enlightenment,* because it moves and while it remains in motion, does not exhaust itself in the perverse effects noted by the *apocalyptic* observers of the technocratic culture industry who have undertaken to demystify the non-critical image of neo-capitalism that those *integrated into the system* unceasingly describe and popularize. In any case, an embodied and socialized culture has an ever more central role to play in the elaboration of a future for poor nations.

Let us review the semantic areas occupied by the *colo-cultus* dyad, recalling that each element can convey material or symbolic meanings, depending on context:

1) The economic applications of the term *colo* represent the active, energetic capacities of a society in transition, transplanting itself into a new context. Cultivation of the land, after all, was a fundamental strategy for survival during the Roman period and in medieval Europe. Latin, an eminently rural language, created the expression *colere vitam* (literally, "to cultivate life"), which is used in one of Plautus's comedies simply in the sense of "to live." *Egomet vix vitam colo:* I myself am barely cultivating life (*Rudens*, I, 5, 25). Or in Brazilian slang, *vou gramando* (I continue laying down grass, that is, working/suffering). How can one separate the social from its natural metaphor in this last expression? Here life is lived as the product of continual action by the cultivator who, as he labors, in fact cultivates himself.

2) In terms of its religious application, it remembers, it recovers the origins, it reestablishes the individual's connection to a spiritual or cosmic

totality. The cult gives meaning to time, it redeems it from daily entropy and from the death to which each new moment of life consigns the moment that preceded it. *O grave, where is thy victory?* Paul's challenge to death, the great enemy, in his address to the Corinthians is the culmination and distillation of all human beliefs. The cult should not be confused with direct, instrumental manipulation of objects and persons (recall the universal distinction between magic and devotion); the cult, in and of itself, in its pure form and divorced from the powers that attempt to appropriate it for their own ends, signifies respect for the difference and transcendence of others, as well as the desire to break through the limits of one's self and use the power of the soul to overcome the anguish of finite, carnal existence. There are elements of renunciation and oblation in all religious activity, and particularly in the spiritual and moral significance of the cult.

Reverence for ancestors, which is common to African and Amerindian religiosity, and to popular Catholic veneration of saints, merits some specific discussion here. The deceased is simultaneously the absolute other, closed off in immutable silence and removed from economic struggle, and a familiar image that stands in vigil over the homes of the living: when called upon by them, the deceased can give welcome comfort amid present-day suffering. The community makes use of a series of rituals and prayers (that consecrate, as opposed to substitute for, everyday practices) to access the power of the deceased. Far from being mutually exclusive, manual and religious labor complement each other in traditional societies. *Ora et labora* (pray and work) was the motto of the Order of Saint Benedict, one of the first monastic communities of the Middle Ages.

35

II. Amplified Reflection and Contradiction in the Colonizing Process

Colonization refigures the three orders—cultivation, cult, and culture—within a dialectical structure.

The order of cultivation, first of all: the movements of migration and population reinforce the basic principle, common to all societies, of humanity's dominion over nature. New lands and resources are exposed to the invaders' greed. The predatory, mercantile impetus for economic development is reignited, leading to accelerated accumulation of wealth, generally with considerable implications for the system of international exchange. We can appreciate what the relentless Latin American sugar cultivation and mineral extraction meant for the European bourgeoisie of the mercantile age. If we equate the increased circulation of goods with the idea of progress, then we cannot deny that New World colonization worked to modernize European commercial networks during the sixteenth, seventeenth, and eighteenth centuries. In this context, the colonial economy was a product of and stimulus for metropolitan markets during the long period between the last phase of feudalism and the beginning of the Industrial Revolution.

Karl Marx provides two obligatory citations for my discussion of this issue:

> The discovery of gold and silver in America, the extirpation, enslavement and entombment in mines of the aboriginal population, the beginning of the conquest and looting of the East Indies, the turning of Africa into a warren for the commercial hunting of black-skins, signalised the rosy dawn of the era of capitalist production. These idyllic proceedings are the chief momenta of primitive accumulation. On their heels treads the commercial war of the European nations, with the globe for a theatre. (1: 823)[vii]

> Merchants' capital in its supremacy everywhere stands for a system of rob-

bery, and its development, among the trading nations of old and new times, is always connected with plundering, piracy, snatching of slaves, conquest of colonies. See Carthage, Rome, and later Venetians, Portuguese, Dutch, etc. (3: 389-90)

Marx clearly saw that the colonizing process was not limited to its modernizing effect as an eventual stimulant of world capitalism. In fact, colonization promoted or reinvented archaic systems of labor, beginning with the extermination or enslavement of the native inhabitants of areas of greatest economic interest. Violent forms of social interaction are implanted in the colonized area as a result of an occupation oriented toward short-term resource extraction. The distinct models of the Mexican or Peruvian *encomienda*, the *engenho* of the Brazilian northeast, the Antillean plantation, and the *hacienda* of the River Plate region all played host to these forms of social relationship. Without entering into the difficult question of the conceptual nature of the colonial economy (was it feudal, semi-feudal, capitalist?), we may safely note the continual state of coercion and strict dependence to which Amerindians, Afro-Latins, and *mestiços* were subjected in the varied models of production implemented in Portuguese and Spanish America. The European conquerors tightened the mechanisms of exploitation and control in the name of more efficient and more secure resource extraction. This regressive deployment of tactical tools seems to have been a structural feature of colonization, with the European's dual role as New World colonizer and mercantile agent not exactly promoting the humanization of labor conditions.

The expansion of modern commercial capitalism, stimulated by the promise of conquering new lands, had the contradictory yet inevitable effect of brutalizing the day-to-day life of the colonized, of subjecting them to a bloody and primitive existence. The genocide of the Aztecs and of the Incas, the work of Cortés and Pizarro, was only the first act. There were many to follow—for instance, Argentina's murderous mid-century *conquista del desierto* (conquest of the desert), at the expense of Patagonian Amerindians and mestizos:

One could be paid in English currency for the ears *of an Indian,* but since it was quickly found that many of the Amerindians who had lost their ears were still alive, the more effective measure was taken of paying for a pair of

an *Indian's testicles*. The authors of this genocide, many of whom were foreign adventurers, accumulated incredible fortunes. Others, finding themselves in the possession of stolen lands, rose into the ranks of nobility.
(Galich 390)[viii]

As the historian Manuel Galich comments:

Why this desire for land? It was clearly in order to exponentially increase
the number of cattle, since the value of cattle had grown exponentially in
the English market. Cattle were no longer only good for leather, their fat,
their horns, and their hooves. Beef had also become big business ever since
the Frenchman Tellier had figured out how to preserve meat through refrigeration, and export companies like The River Plate Fresh Co. and La Negra
had been formed as a result. It is notable and worthy of further reflection
that the period of the *conquista del desierto* coincided with the opening of
the international beef market and the invention of refrigeration (1876). This
was a progressive move on capitalism's part, without a doubt.

Those who accompanied the cycle of the Iberian conquests did not
ignore the extent of the crimes committed. The Dominican friar Bartolomé
de Las Casas published his *Brevísima relación de la destrucción de las
Indias* (A Very Brief Account of the Devastation of the Indies) in Seville in
1552, in which he put the number of Amerindians killed between 1492 and
1542 at fifteen million. And Michel de Montaigne, a probable reader of Las
Casas and the first of the secular humanists, recorded these fiery words in
Book III of his *Essais* (1588):

Whoever else has ever rated trade and commerce at such a price? So many
cities razed to the ground, so many nations wiped out, so many millions of
individuals put to the sword, and the most beautiful and the richest part of
the world shattered, on behalf of the pearls-and-pepper business!
Tradesmen's victories! At least ambition and political strife never led men
against men to such acts of horrifying enmity and to such pitiable disasters.
(1031)[ix]

In Brazil, barbaric abuse of the environment and of people accompanied the march of colonization, both in the sugar-growing zone and in the

backlands of the *bandeirantes,* bringing about the burning of forests and the murder or enslavement of native populations. Even Gilberto Freyre, an apologist for Portuguese colonization in Brazil and elsewhere, wrote that "sugar eliminated the Indian." Today we might add that cattle, soy, and sugarcane expel small and marginal landholders. The expansionist project of the 1970s and 80s was, and continues to be, nothing more than an equally cruel extension of colonial-era military and economic incursions.4

In his *Essai sur la colonisation* (1907), Carl Siger offers a curious defense of colonial methods, which he considers authentic "safety valves" (*soupapes de sûreté*) for the metropolises:

> Les pays neufs sont un vaste champ ouvert aux activités individuelles, vio-
> lentes, qui, dans les métropoles, se heurteraient à certains préjugés, à une
> conception sage et réglée de la vie et qui, aux colonies, peuvent se dévelop-
> per plus librement et mieux affirmer, par suite, leur valeur. Ainsi les
> colonies peuvent, à un certain point, servir de soupapes de sûreté à la
> société moderne. Cette utilité serait-elle la seule, elle est immense.[x]

40

To Marx, an economy subject to European capitalism but based on slave labor seemed an *anomaly*. He says as much in a revealing passage from his *Pre-Capitalist Economic Formations*: "If we now talk of planta-tion-owners in America as capitalists, if they *are* capitalists, this is due to the fact that they exist as anomalies within a world market based upon free labour" (119). To be exact, the term *anomaly,* which Marx applies to America's slave-based plantation economy, presupposes the existence of a norm (*nomos*) or an exemplary standard. In Marx's case, this standard was the mode of capitalist production in mid-nineteenth century England, a mode conditioned precisely on the forced transition from agricultural servitude to salaried labor. At the beginning of the paragraph quoted above, Marx affirms categorically that "[t]he production of capitalists and wage-labourers is therefore a major product of the process by which capi-tal turns itself into values."

The long duration of a system of *non-salaried* labor on the Brazilian *fazendas* and the plantations of the U.S. South appeared to the author of *Capital,* writing during the second half of the nineteenth century, as an aberration, a holdover from an earlier age doomed to disappear with the worldwide growth of openly capitalistic productive forces.

However, if our objective is to understand the peculiar internal workings of colonialism, the reality is that the *anomaly* of slave labor was long-lasting and represented a formative influence in colonial society's social and psychological existence. As Marx wrote in another context, "the civilized horrors of over-work are grafted onto the barbaric horrors of slavery" (*Capital* 1: 340). Brazilian political practices were formed in the simultaneously modern and retrograde context of colonial Brazil's slave-based economy. If Marx was correct in his use of the term "anomaly," then it falls to us to study the phenomenology of an anomalous situation.

In general terms, it is possible to describe colonial Brazil as a socio-economic formation whose basic characteristics were as follows:

1) The colony was dominated by a class of landowners whose interests were linked to groups of European merchants, particularly the traffickers of African slaves. Given this structural dependence on external forces, the prospect of an internally dynamic capitalist economy in the colonized zone became totally unrealistic. The expression *colonial capitalism* should be understood in terms of colonial-metropolitan commercial interaction.

2) The labor force was basically composed of slaves, and the economy of the time can therefore be characterized as a system of *colonial slave-holding* (*escravismo colonial*), the concept used by Jacob Gorender to describe the Brazilian, Antillean, and southern U.S. plantation economies.

3) The alternative to slavery was not the transition to salaried labor, but the prospect of escaping to a *quilombo* (an Afro-Brazilian maroon settlement). Law, labor, and oppression were the interrelated guiding forces of colonial slavery. The slaves who were freed by their masters, which became more common after the peak of the colonial mines, faced the alternatives of a difficult life as subsistence farmers working marginal land or as subaltern *agregados* (subordinate, poorly remunerated plantation fixtures who outlived even the abolition of slavery). Regardless, the life of a free Afro-Brazilian amounted to a condition of dependence.

4) The political structure linked the interests of rural landowners to local representative chambers composed of *the gentlemen of the community*, that is, property holders. But the chambers' sphere of influence was limited, with the king nominating governors for four-year terms. The governor, invested with both military and administrative powers, presided over the local armed forces and the *Juntas da Fazenda e da Justiça* (Commerce and Justice Committees), following the criteria established by the Crown

and expressed in royal decrees, letters, and directives. The *juntas* were composed of royal officials: *provedores* (administrators), *ouvidores* (judges), *procuradores* (attorneys), and during the period of the mines, *intendentes* (mine administrators). They were controlled from Lisbon and specifically, from 1642 onward, by the *Conselho Ultramarino* (Overseas Council). From 1696, even municipal chambers were subject to metropolitan interference, with Portugal nominating *juízes de fora* (outside judges) whose powers superseded those of local, municipally elected judges. Historians have stressed the very limited sphere of action of local chambers under the Portuguese kingdom's statutes and laws: one of the results was the tension between local oligarchies and an increasingly centralizing Crown, which would contribute to the political crisis that began in the late eighteenth century. With Brazilian independence in 1822, the authority and authoritarian tendencies of local oligarchies were able to assert themselves, and were formally legitimized by the presence of *bacharéis* (elite men trained in law) in parliament and in the provincial assemblies.[xi]

5) The exercise of citizenship was doubly limited: by an authoritarian state and by internal power dynamics. Throughout colonial Latin America, representative government was practically nonexistent, a situation that remained virtually unchanged (in quantitative terms, at least) with political independence in the first years of the nineteenth century. In imperial Brazil, an indirect, census-based electoral system proved ineffective to counter administrative centralization.

6) The lay clergy was tied both to large rural landowners and to the Crown, on which it depended economically and legally through the patronage system. Hence the prevalence of priests tied to specific *fazendas* or those who doubled as colonial functionaries. It is only when the colonial pact enters a crisis period, between the final years of the eighteenth and the first quarter of the nineteenth century, that liberal and radical priests begin to appear.

7) Religious orders, and especially the Jesuits, committed to the practices of a supranational Church, remained invested in the project of administering Amerindian missions. This possibility was opened at the onset of colonization, when the Portuguese colonizer's Christianizing role was a broadly accepted idea. Over time, the missions were limited to the margins and weak points of the system, and would in the long term succumb to the pressures of *bandeirantes* and the colonial army. The Jesuits

would then be offered the alternative opportunity of ministering to the children of elite families as humanistic educators.

8) Intellectual culture was rigorously stratified, allowing for social mobility only in exceptional cases of educational patronage that did not challenge the general rule. Mastery of the alphabet, which was reserved for the few, served as a dividing line between official culture and popular life. Day-to-day manifestations of colonial-era popular culture were organized and reproduced beyond the pale of writing.

9) The production of popular culture was able to take place either in enclaves seen today, retrospectively, as archaic or rustic or at the margins of certain erudite or semi-erudite codes derived from the European arts: for example, in music, in popular festivals, and in religious imagery. The *romance de cordel,* a form of marginal production, was late in making its appearance due to the barriers to literacy and printing that prevailed during the colonial period.[5]

In a brief synthesis, it is possible to relate Brazil's formative colonial development as follows: economically, to the interests of slave traders and sugar and gold merchants; and politically, to absolutist metropolitan rule and to local authoritarianism, which engendered modes of social interaction that were patriarchal and stratified among the elites and based on slavery or dependency among the subaltern.

III. The Cult-Culture Dialectic within the Colonial Condition

The key factor for considering life in colonial Brazil as a network of values and meanings is precisely the complex alliance between an agricultural and mercantile system oriented toward the European economic machine and a domestic condition that was traditional, if not frankly archaic, in its mores and politics.

I distinguish between the terms *system* and *condition* so as to sound clearly the chords of this tune that some have perceived as rightful and harmonious and others as dissonant and discordant. I understand system as an objectively articulated totality. The *colonial system*, as a long-lasting historical reality, has been studied in the Brazilian context from a variety of structural perspectives by such eminent scholars as Caio Prado Jr., Nelson Werneck Sodré, Celso Furtado, Fernando Novais, Maria Sylvia Carvalho Franco and Jacob Gorender.[xii]

Economic life in Brazil during the first three centuries of Portuguese colonization depended on mechanisms that can be quantified because they are translatable into amounts of production and circulation, that is, into numbers that represent goods and labor. Long before the genesis of quantitative history, the poet Gregório de Matos, in a harsh sonnet dedicated to the city of Salvador da Bahia at the end of the seventeenth century, spoke of a *máquina mercante,* literally a ship of merchandise, an expression that can be extended metonymically to the entire machinery of colonial commerce.[6]

The formation of the system required reciprocal interaction of trade and slavery, monopoly and monoculture. At the international level, the back-and-forth flow of colonial merchandise was subject to market fluctuations and to economic competition among metropolitan states. In sum, the system as it was reproduced in Brazil, and as it was tied to the economies of the European center, occupied opposing sides of the same figurative coin.

The term *condition* comprehends a more diffuse set of experiences than the regular movements of production and trade described by *system*. To speak of a *condition* implies ways of living and surviving. It is not coincidental that we speak naturally of a *human condition*, but never of a *human system*.

While the conditions of master and slave implied distinct roles to be played within the sugar economy (which we may uncover through a functional analysis of its system of production), they cannot be reduced to the actions those roles entailed. A person's *condition* comprehends multiple, concrete forms of interpersonal, subjective existence—memories, dreams, the daily marks made on the heart and mind, the manner of one's birth, physical sustenance, living and sleeping conditions, ways of loving, crying, praying and singing, and the circumstances surrounding one's death and burial.

Earlier in this analysis I recalled some of the key studies that have contributed to the understanding of the colonial system. As for the colonial condition, Gilberto Freyre's and Sérgio Buarque de Holanda's classic studies are obligatory reading. In texts like *Casa-grande & senzala* (*The Masters and the Slaves*) and *Sobrados e mucambos* (*The Mansions and the Shanties*), Freyre dedicated himself to developing an existential anthropology of Brazil's northeastern sugar economy. Following his own synthesis of the process of colonization in *Raízes do Brasil* (Roots of Brazil), Buarque offered a detailed and elegant description of the daily life of the *sertanejos,* the "luso-Tupi" inhabitants of Brazil's backlands, in *Caminhos e fronteiras* (Paths and Frontiers), a volume that provides a pioneering analysis of our material culture.[7]

In their treatment of familial and clan behavior, Freyre's and Buarque's essays suggest a psycho-cultural interpretation of Brazil's past. This reading of our history is based on the general hypothesis that the Portuguese conqueror brought with him to Brazil certain recurring character traits, which Buarque termed *psychological determinants*. They include individualism, which he qualifies as an *extreme exaltation of the personality,* an adventurer's spirit (hence the Luso-Brazilian *ethic of adventure* as opposed to an *ethic of labor*), our *natural tendencies toward restlessness and disorder*, cordiality, a sensual sentimentality exercised freely in what Freyre classified as *polygamous patriarchalism*, social plasticity, versatility, and finally, a tendency toward miscegenation that harkens back to the

Portuguese interactions with the Moors and that was intensified by a *lack of racial pride*, a trait that appears in both scholars' analyses.

When the various patterns of the so-called Luso-African and Luso-Tupi *assimilation* are seen through this psycho-cultural lens, the structural features of enslavement and violence become relegated to a subdued or implicit background, though they were in reality a constant of colonial history, as much a part of the northeastern *engenhos* and *quilombos* as of the *bandeirantes'* expeditions and the Jesuit missions of the South.[8]

Having fully acknowledged the value of these masterly texts, it may be helpful to offer a semantic correction to terms like *assimilation* (Freyre) and expressions such as the *process of successful acclimatization and cultural solidarity* (Buarque) when these are applied to contacts between the colonizers and the colonized. This vocabulary may lead less informed readers to assume that the peoples who interacted during colonization became similar to each other, and dealt with each other on *friendly* terms, as illustrated by their miscegenated daily routines, diets, sexual habits, production techniques, modes of transportation, etc. It is instructive to reread passages from *Casa-grande & senzala* and *Raízes do Brasil* that deal with how plantation owners and *bandeirantes* were compelled to adopt African and indigenous customs in response to the conditions of a new life in the tropics. The majority of these passages describe examples of sexual and nutritional enjoyment of Africans and their culture by the planter class or the simple appropriation of Tupi-Guarani habits by the Portuguese in São Paulo. The colonist literally *incorporates* African and indigenous material and cultural resources when, driven by self-interest and pursuit of pleasure, he takes by force the labor of black or Amerindian slaves, as he takes the bodies of their women, their well-tested recipes for planting and cooking, and by extension, the general, indispensable know-how that allows them to survive in a rustic environment.

The use of the bodies of others and the appropriation of their bodily techniques, ably described by Marcel Mauss, do not make for properly reciprocal acculturation. The most we can say is that the colonizers took excellent advantage of their relationships with Amerindians and Africans.

In *Casa-grande & senzala*, Freyre insists on celebrating the northeastern plantation owner who, free from prejudice, mingled fruitfully and *polygamously* with female slaves, thereby providing the world with an example of racially democratic tolerance. For his part, Buarque attributes

47

colonial-era miscegenation to the Portuguese colonizer's unique *lack of racial pride*. Even here we must qualify the argument so as to avoid sliding from a dubious social psychology into an ideology that ends up celebrating the European victor. The conqueror's libido, which nearly always exercised itself in an exclusively physical capacity, was more phallocratic than democratic: the female slaves impregnated by the plantation owners were not elevated *ipso facto* to the category of wife or *senhora de engenho* (plantation mistress), nor were the children that resulted from these fleeting encounters treated as the equals of those considered legitimate heirs to the property. Rare, late exceptions to this rule can be cited, but the anecdotal material serves merely to confirm the larger truth. Intense sexual and reproductive activity does not necessarily equate to social generosity.

In Buarque's highly erudite texts, a subtle sublimation of *bandeirante* activity, presented as the natural outgrowth of the processes of Portuguese acclimatization to Brazil, downplays the aggression and conflict that objectively characterized the *paulista* incursions into the interior and the indigenous and Jesuit opposition they faced.[9] In arguing his position, the author of *Raízes do Brasil* subscribes to Júlio de Mesquita Filho's apology for Portuguese colonization in his *Ensaios sul-americanos* (South American Essays), and goes as far as to compare the plasticity of the Portuguese to St. John the Evangelist's figurative grain of wheat, which sacrifices itself in order to bear much fruit (188).[xiii] How could black slaves held prisoner in the country and the Amerindians hunted in the forests have imagined that the plantation masters and the *bandeirantes* were completing some sacrificial rite in which the ultimate victim was not black or Amerindian but white?

The elements of material culture that are cited *ad nauseam* as evidence of the colonizer's adaptation to the ways of the colonized should not be made to prove more than they can handle. They illustrate the uses and abuses to which the Portuguese subjected Amerindians and Africans, both at the level of global economy and in daily material and corporeal practice. Why should we idealize what occurred? Should Brazilian scholars compete with other colonized peoples to decide who was *best colonized?* I do not believe that this careless and often naïve game of comparisons, stacked to favor *our* colonizer, can lead to an adequate understanding of the process.

We must ask if, along with the most evident of the adaptations alluded to above, the forces of cult and culture (and the art that feeds on both), succeeded, through their capacity to grant meaning to life, in addressing that which routine left unfulfilled or untouched.

The reproduction of a certain set of habits certainly helped to prop up the colonial structure, but was the consuming, producing, and trading machine of colonization able to respond to the full range of values, ideals, dreams, and desires issuing from the pasts or projected, at least in potential form, into the futures of both colonizers and colonized? In other words: was colonization a process defined by moments of fusion and *construction*, which ultimately balanced out material wants and symbolic forms, immediate needs and imaginary worlds; or did colonization produce also, besides a machinery of interlocking parts, a dialectic of ruptures, differences, and contrasts?

Marx's words on the role of religion in oppressed societies help explain the tendencies of certain social groups toward the imaginary expression of their desires: religion is the "heart of a heartless world and the soul of soulless conditions" (*Critique* 131). A society's symbolic labor can reveal the dark consequences of forced labor and the search for new, freer forms of existence. This is much like the platonic Eros, who as the child of Wealth and Poverty is in fact neither, but rather the will to free oneself from the yoke of the present and to ascend to the realm of imperishable values. Popular rituals, music, and religious imagery of the colonial era are signs of this desired state. In certain of these cultural manifestations we can detect the presence of both the weight of the past and the hope for the future within the links of the tightly binding chain of oppression. The colonial condition, like the colonial system, is reflexive and contradictory.

T.S. Eliot, addressing the broader dynamic between colony and metropolis, writes the following:

> The culture which develops on the new soil must therefore be bafflingly alike and different from the parent culture: it will be complicated sometimes by whatever relations are established with some native race, and further by immigration from other than the original source. In this way, peculiar types of *culture-sympathy* and *culture-clash* appear, between the areas populated by colonisation and the countries of Europe from which the migrants came. (64; my emphasis)

There are cases of successful transplants, long-lasting grafts, and felicitous encounters; and there are sounds of dissonant chords that reveal poorly resolved contrasts and maladjusted overlappings. Colonial history is made from both empathy and antipathy.

In a typically perceptive passage, Alphonse Dupront alerts us to the limitations of a historiographical and ethnological language that makes use of *acculturation, assimilation,* and *cultural encounter,* broad terms that are able to express (or to conceal) opposing meanings:

> There are encounters that kill. Should we say the same, with a kind of black humor, of cultural exchanges? Anthropologists would respond with assimilation. But isn't this too a form of black humor? Should we describe processes of death and processes of life using the same verbal sign, like the liars we are? (89)

The transposition of European norms of behavior and language onto the New World yielded varied results. At first glance, colonial literate culture seems to reproduce the European model without exception; but when confronted with the figure of the Amerindian, it is inspired or even forced to invent. Let the first acculturating agent in colonial Brazil, the Jesuit friar José de Anchieta, serve as an example: when he composed his poem to the Virgin Mary while being held hostage by the Tamoios on the beach of Iperoígue, feeling the need to purify himself, he wrote in classical Latin.[10] The same Anchieta learned the Tupi language, and sang and prayed to the angels and saints of medieval Catholicism in Tupi in the plays he composed for the *curumins*.[11] In the first case, Anchieta used the epic, an ancient literary form elevated by the Italian Renaissance, to give shape to the substance of a colonial situation. In the second, he changed codes in the interest of his evangelizing mission—not because his message had changed, but rather his recipients. This new public, which was participating actively in a new, unique form of theater, required a language that could not be that and only that of the colonizer.

Further, Anchieta made use of a strangely syncretistic imagery, neither exclusively Catholic nor purely Tupi-Guarani, when he created mythical figures named *karaibebé*, literally *flying prophets*. His indigenous audience might see these as the heralds of the Land without Evil, while Christians would identify them as the angelic messengers of the Bible. And in Anchieta's plays Tupansy, the mother of Tupã, took on characteristics of

Our Lady.[12] Culture-as-reflection and culture-as-creation walked arm in arm.

The peculiar dynamism of the Jesuits in Brazil, who were compelled to faithfully observe the vows made by their order in Counter-Reformation-era Iberia, should be accompanied up close. There would come a time when the cross and the sword, which had disembarked together from the caravels onto the shore, drifted apart, became hostile to one another, and ultimately waged battle for the shared good: the bodies and souls of the Amerindians.

The fight to the death between the *bandeirantes* of São Paulo and the Company of Jesus, which resulted in the Jesuits' final defeat in the mid-eighteenth century, speaks eloquently of how an unspoken opposition can explode into the open when missionary paternalism and the colonists' naked exploitation of the Amerindians can no longer be balanced.

Anchieta considered the Portuguese his primary opponents in cate-chizing the Amerindians; as he stated,

> the Portuguese are the source of the greatest impediments, the first of which is their lack of dedication to saving the Indians [...] Rather, they con-sider them savages. What most frightens the Indians and causes them to flee from the Portuguese, and as a consequence from the churches, is the tyranny the Portuguese exercise over them, forcing them to serve their entire lives as slaves, separating wives from husbands, parents from chil-dren, chaining them, selling them, etc. [...] These needless injustices caused the destruction of the churches that had been established, and are the cause of the great perdition of the Indians now in their power. (334)

Denouncing the *mamelucos* (children of whites and Amerindians) under the control of the patriarch João Ramalho,[13] Anchieta wrote:

> they most hatefully persecuted us, using all means and methods to do us harm, threatening us with death, but most especially working to nullify the doctrine we used to instruct the Indians, thereby causing them to hate us. If this deadly contagion is not eliminated, not only will the conversion of the unfaithful fail to progress, but it will weaken day by day and inevitably decline. (334)

Such was the first century of missionary activity in Brazil. Anchieta's fears were confirmed by the facts, as illustrated in his description of the flight of the Amerindians from São Tomé:

> Suddenly all the people of São Tomé rose up, rebelling such that the Devil seemed to be walking among them. In the streets they cried out: "Let us flee, let us flee from the Portuguese who are coming." Father Gaspar Lourenço, witnessing this upheaval, gathered them together and made them understand how grave it would be if they abandoned the church because of the lies told to them. Crying, they responded: "We flee neither from the church nor from you, and if you wish to go with us, we will live with you in the forest or the backlands. We see that God's law is good, but these Portuguese do not leave us in peace, and if you can see how the few of them that walk among us steal our brothers and sisters, what can be expected when the rest come and make slaves of us, our women, and our children?" With many tears and much emotion, some of them described the threats and showed the wounds they had received in the homes of the Portuguese. (375)

52

Anchieta's narrative foregrounds the sharp contrast between predatory colonization and the apostolic mission, which initially were linked of necessity. All the evidence indicates that these were distinct projects whose moments of reconciliation were invariably fleeting and diplomatic, but whose inner dynamic forces were such as to lead them to open confrontation with each other.

The seventeenth century in Brazil is marked by conflicts between colonists and Jesuits, from Grão-Pará and Maranhão, where Antônio Vieira worked and served as a witness, to São Paulo and, most dramatically, to the Missions of the Sete Povos do Uruguai (the Seven Settlements of Uruguay).[14] However, the tension between Church and State would not be limited to the followers of Ignatius of Loyola.

Ecclesiastical power frequently entered into confrontation with civil interests and laws. While the motives for conflict were varied, the tutelage of the Amerindians appeared as a causal factor on more than one occasion. See, for example, the problems faced by the prelates of Rio de Janeiro. The first occupant of the office, Father Bartolomeu Simões Pereira, died of poisoning in 1598; the second, Father João da Costa, was persecuted, expelled from the city, and removed from his position by a colonial court; the third,

Father Mateus Aborim, was also the victim of poisoning; the fourth and fifth prelates made the prudent decision not to assume their office; the sixth, the reverend Lourenço de Mendonça, was forced to flee to Portugal after escaping a fire that had engulfed his home, set by locals who had exploded a barrel of gunpowder in his yard; the seventh, Father Antônio de Mariz Loureiro (perhaps a relative of José de Alencar's Marizes), faced such opposition that he retreated to the captaincy of Espírito Santo, where he lost his mind after an attempted poisoning.[15] I must pass over the story of the eighth prelate, the famous Dr. Manoel de Sousa e Almada, since the sources are intensely divided on the matter of his guilt or innocence: the fact remains that his palace was damaged by cannon fire, a Bahian court absolved the aggressors and, as if this were not enough, charged Almada with paying for the court case;[xiv] Machado de Assis parodied the affair in his heroic-comic poem "Almada."[16]

This struggle is at the same time material and cultural, and is therefore political. If we are interested in tracing the development of ideas, not in and of themselves but in relation to the existential horizons of their authors, then we can identify two discourses at work in colonial writing: an organic discourse and an ecclesiastical or traditional discourse, to use Gramsci's felicitous distinction.

The organic discourse is produced in connection with the actions of the colonial enterprise and is often preferred by the colonial agents themselves. Witness, for instance, Pero Vaz de Caminha, the scribe attached to the armada that discovered Brazil; Gabriel Soares de Sousa, a plantation owner and New Christian who was a hands-on informant, as well as an accurate and precious one ("étonnant," in Alfred Métraux's judgment); Ambrósio Fernandes Brandão, the attentive and engaged chronicler who wrote the *Diálogos das grandezas do Brasil* (Dialogs on the Great Things of Brazil); and Antonil, an author who hid behind an anagram and discreetly called himself the Anonymous Tuscan, and who indiscreetly told of the whereabouts and the worth of the colony's natural resources in his *Cultura e opulência do Brasil* (Culture and Opulence of Brazil). Antonil had a modern, pragmatic mind, and probed deeply into the quantifiable details of colonial production despite his Jesuit cassock. Finally there was Azeredo Coutinho, a bishop and Mason who, as the nineteenth century was dawning, called for preserving slavery in the interest of Pernambuco's sugar economy and the well-being of the Portuguese Crown. In all these cases, and without regard to the individual's lay or ecclesiastical status, we find a frank and consistent dedication to exploring, organizing, and commanding in the colonial sphere.

The other discourse, which derives from a pre-capitalist ethic, resists the mercantile system even as it resides in its interstices. Though it lives off the system, issuing as it does from the quills of high officials, nobles, and religious figures, it shows little gratitude to the source from which it derives its privilege of leisure and relief from the cares of business, preferring to castigate the colonists for their hunger for profit and for their shortage of Christian selflessness. This is the message of Gregório de Matos's moralizing satires against the foreign merchant (*o sagaz Brichote*) and the nouveau riche usurer who claims aristocratic roots (*o fidalgo caramuru*), and of Antônio Vieira's somber homilies, with their Baroquely convoluted separation between a defense of good commercial practices and a condemnation of the abuses of slavery, which in fact were at the heart of that very commerce. The same sentiment can be seen vacilating, in Basílio da Gama's *Uraguai*, between, on the one hand, the author's glorification of colonial military force and Gomes Freire de Andrade's resetting of the overseas balance of power, and, on the other, his poeticizing of the rebellious indigenous savages, ultimately the only people who are considered worthy of singing the song of freedom.[17]

Colonial writing does not constitute an undifferentiated whole: it gestures toward practical knowledge, oriented toward the hard demands of the Western market system, while it also aspires toward its counterpoint, where obscure utopian dreams of a naturally Christian humanity fuse with the values of liberty and equality that were being very slowly advanced by the rising bourgeoisie. Whenever we are alerted to the presence of these counter-ideological gestures, we discover that the present either looks back to the past, and is linked to the *cult*, or that it looks toward an ideal future, and responds to *culture*.

Ghosts of this old, intermittently appearing dream haunt Vieira's millenarian tirades, the missionaries' idealized descriptions of the Sete Povos, Aleijadinho's statues of suffering but indomitable prophets, and the escapist landscapes of the *árcades* of Minas Gerais.[18] Of course there are many types of utopia, and it is only by analyzing each given context that we can see how they came into being, and toward and against whom they were addressed.

But where do the varied fantasies of utopia put down roots in the rocky soil of colonial culture? The Neapolitan philosopher Giambattista Vico characterized collective human fantasies in terms of "extended or compounded memory."[xv] A people's shared past is freely reconfigured by each succeeding generation, taking on new meanings. Memory gleans countless themes and images from a more or less remote spiritual history, but the conflicts of the here-and-now compel it to give a defined form to the open, polyvalent legacy provided by cult and culture.

In Vieira's messianic words, the Bible was made to defend the Jews. The same Bible defended the Jesuit himself against the forces of the Inquisition, who also drew on the holy scripture to make their case against him. Rabbis, Jesuits, Dominicans: all were experts in scriptural exegesis. The prophets Isaiah, Daniel, and Jeremiah supplied the missionary Vieira with the words to castigate the slaveholders of Maranhão for their greed, even as he endorsed Paul's oft-abused argument for servants to remain loyal to their masters in advising the Portuguese king against a mediated solution to the conflict with the revolting *quilombolas* of Palmares.[19] The great rhetorician drew on the treasury of shared memory, whether to argue for the slaves or to defend capital. The past helps compose the forms of the present, but it is the present that picks old or new garments from the chest of the past.

What a strange religion, half Baroque and half mercantile! Religion that denounces the victors and then leaves the victims to their fate, and that abandons a fragile, defenseless holy word to the scheming designs of the powerful, who plunder it for all they want.

Art, whether sacred or profane, redraws the profile of tradition. The profusion of tortured devotional images hammered out by the Iberian Counter-Reformation inspired the mature Aleijadinho's prophetic figures at Congonhas do Campo, whose appearance, according to some, foreshadows the *mineiros'* rebellion and its bloody suppression by the Crown. During the same turn-of-the-century period our Arcadian poets would draw on Virgil and Horace to fill with woodland flowers the tropical plain surrounding the Ribeirão do Carmo (Carmo creek), which they sang of with a classical lyre. And in the Vila Rica that clings to the hillside, Virgilian shadows fell broadly from the golden hills.

Fantasy amounts to memory, either expanded upon or compounded. To try to understand colonial culture in its symbolic forms is to deal with the coexistence of a culture of the day-to-day, born of and developed from the practices of migrants and natives alike, with another culture that confronts the machinery of daily routine with the ever-changing faces of the past and future, sometimes juxtaposed and sometimes transforming each other.

Vieira denounced the cruelties of slavery in the northeastern *engenhos* using a universalizing, prophetic and evangelical discourse (it would be anachronistic, when referring to his time, to speak of liberal or, especially, democratic principles of later centuries). Christianity's basic message, that all men are children of the same God and are therefore brothers, contradicts, in principle, pseudo-arguments that have been marshaled to defend colonial particularity. These arguments have been presented in a utilitarian, fatalistic, and even racist language: the self-interested speech of the oppressor rooted in the organic reasons driving conquest, which reasserted itself on a planetary scale, with little variation, until the last phase of colonial imperialism beginning at the end of the nineteenth century.[xvi]

In Brazil, praising plantation owners, *bandeirantes*, captains, and governors-general—in short, the Crown and its collection of servants and bureaucrats—was the vulgar but inexhaustible rhetorical strategy of the Bahian academies, the *Esquecidos* (Forgotten) and the *Renascidos* (Reborn), as well as the favored theme of the genealogists of São Paulo and Pernambuco, centers of the Brazilian nobility since the eighteenth century.[20] This discourse drove also epic texts composed in various periods: Bento Teixeira's *Prosopopéia,* a Camonian pastiche written at the beginning of the seventeenth century and dedicated to the hereditary captain of Pernambuco, Jorge de Albuquerque Coelho; Brother Manuel Calado's *O valoroso Lucideno,* which celebrates in verse and prose the achievements of João Fernandes Vieira, a Portuguese magnate who owned five sugar plantations and mills and helped lead the resistance against the Dutch in northeastern Brazil;[21] Brother José de Santa Rita Durão's *Caramuru,* written in honor of Diogo Álvares Correia, the patriarch of Bahia; and finally, Cláudio Manuel da Costa's *Vila Rica,* a poem written to celebrate the civil order imposed by Antônio Dias in Minas Gerais. The last two texts belong to the neoclassical Luso-Brazilian literary corpus read (and in part, misread) during the Second Reign by the Brazilian Romantics who were in search of prototypical examples of the official nationalism they were working to construct.[22] Theirs was a misinterpretation: despite neoclassicism's celebration of the landscape and its chronicling of local life, the eighteenth-century epos cannot be dislodged from the colonial context. Its tendency toward localism, which was quite visible in Pernambuco after the expulsion of the Dutch and in post-*bandeirista* São Paulo, was tied to elite families' self-fashioning as local nobilities. These same families would eventually constitute the ruling class of the future Brazilian nation-state.

To recapitulate: two rhetorical tendencies were present in colonial letters, generally running parallel, but sometimes in tangential contact with each other. These were a humanistic-Christian rhetoric and that of the intellectual spokesmen for the agro-mercantile system. While the first sought to join culture and cult, utopia and tradition, the second firmly placed writing in the service of the efficient operation of the colonial economic machine, articulating culture and *colo*. Placed side by side, these two languages, one grounded in humanism and the other in economic concerns, seem to contradict each other. However, if we examine them closely and in their respective contexts, we can locate more than one instance of mutual approximation.

IV. Vox Populi vs. Colonial Epos:
A Camonian Parenthesis

> Modern colonialism started with the fifteenth-century
> voyages of the Portuguese along the west coast of
> Africa, which in 1498 brought Vasco da Gama to India.
> *International Encyclopedia of the Social Sciences*,
> 1968, vol. 3, entry on "Colonialism"

Ezra Pound once described poets as antennas. In as rich and dense a text as Luís de Camões's epic poem *Os Lusíadas* we can detect the first signs of an ideological contrast that foreshadows the dialectic of colonization. In his poem Camões does more than simply play host to different perspectives; he conceives of the Portuguese campaign of maritime exploration and conquest as an act of violent dismemberment. As an observer and participant, an author and actor in the colonizing adventure, Camões constructs his epic presentation of Vasco da Gama's voyage from a variety of materials, incorporating premonitory visions, exemplary myths, accounts of Atlantic maritime voyages and disasters, and elements of contemporary drama into the text, sometimes embodying these elements in hieratic figures who verge on the allegorical.

Camões's narrator was able to mold the epic substance of his chosen topic into a dialectical opposition at the exact moment of the greatest glorification of the Portuguese. Glory, after all, is at the heart of *Os Lusíadas*: the glory of Dom Manuel, the glory of da Gama, the glory of the heroes of Portugal's maritime explorations of Africa, and the glory of Portugal.

Let us take a close look at the steps that lead up to the crucial hour of the crew's departure for India. Vasco da Gama's speech to the king of Melinde begins in Canto III. The captain narrates the history of Portugal as one of incessant and ultimately victorious armed struggle against the Moors and the Castilian nobility. The House of Aviz[23] emerges from these centuries of combat, and it is precisely D. João I's alliance with the bourgeoisie, or the "people," as described in Canto IV, that allows for a policy of maritime exploration: "que foi buscar na roxa Aurora / os términos, que eu vou buscando agora" ["To touch the rosy fingers of the dawn, / The very quest to which I myself was born"] (IV, 60).

In trying to reach a climax in his apotheotic treatment of da Gama, Camões accelerates the pace of the narrative, bringing the African cycle of the poem to a quick close. The poem's thesis, which is the affirmation of the kingdom's expansionist project, gains the irresistible force of myth. The king D. Manuel, "whose constant/ Passion was to enlarge the kingdom," does not deviate for a minute from "his unique/ Inheritance"; he neither rests in daytime nor at night, with his thoughtful vigil leading to allegorical dreaming, "[w]here imaginings can be so vivid."

About what does Manuel the Fortunate (*O Venturoso*) dream? "Morpheus, in various guises, rose before him." In his dreams the king rises to a great height, from where he can see other worlds and faraway nations. He sees that two great rivers spring from the Far East, flowing through a wild, verdant land, as yet untrodden by human feet. From their waters majestically rise two old men "of venerable appearance." The descriptive beauty of this dreamtime transformation is admirable: the streams of water become the men's hair and beards. Their dark skin indicates that they come from a tropical region, and the "chaplets of grass and nameless fronds" adorning their heads, along with the grave expressions on their faces, point to royal status. Their words to D. Manuel answer the riddle of their mysterious identity: they are the Ganges and the Indus, the sacred rivers of Asia, which flow from heaven to earth to offer their "tribute" to the Portuguese sovereign.

This episode is revealing of certain ideas that are dear to Camões: the size and strangeness of a hostile world, "whose necks were never before yoked," and the fatal power of the Portuguese Crown, to which nature and men from the remotest regions anxiously and even insistently give themselves over.

D. Manuel's dream must be seen as foretelling good fortune, insofar as it participates in the ideological economy of the poem. It is a dream *where imaginings can be so vivid* [in the original, where imaginings are "truer" (*mais certas*)], a phrase that illustrates the role of allegory as a figure fulfilled in the text's conceptual apparatus and ultimate resolution. Indeed, the episode's connection to the *telos* of the poem becomes apparent immediately after the ghosts of the night vanish. D. Manuel awakens and calls upon his loyal counselors (there are always counselors able to determine royal wishes) who dutifully decipher "the figures of his dream." From this moment on there is no time for hesitation, only continuous action: the wise men "resolve at once to equip / A fleet and an intrepid crew" and the *Venturoso* charges Vasco da Gama with leading the expedition.

Once the fog of the dream has lifted, the narrative proceeds in lively and cheerful fashion to the scene of the fleet's departure, in which all the pipes and trumpets of the Camonian muse will sound. A period of celebration, of "noble bustle" and "youthful spirits," begins, with soldiers dressed in many-colored outfits and flags flying high in the wind.

While this is a joyful scene, the emotional climate of the episode is, to the reader's surprise, marked by sadness and foreboding. The sailors' ritual prayer speaks of "prepar[ing] our souls to meet death." Divine favor is petitioned, but God's response is uncertain. The narrative turns to the interior life of the hero, up to this point known only as the monolithic *stalwart commander* dedicated to the glory of the Kingdom:

> Certifico-te, ó Rei, que se contemplo
> Como fui destas praias apartado
> Cheio dentro de dúvida e receio
> Que apenas nos meus olhos ponho o freio. (IV, 87)

> [O King, I tell you, when I reflect
> On how I parted from that shore,
> Tormented by so many doubts and fears,
> Even now it is hard to restrain my tears.]

With this mention of doubt and fear, the narrative has taken its first steps toward the antithetical climax of the episode. In effect, Vasco da Gama does not undertake his spiritual labor in isolation, but is accompanied by a true tragic chorus composed of those staying behind, of the elderly, the invalid, children, and especially women, whose anticipated feelings of longing for their loved ones give way to mourning and finally to open revolt. Da Gama's feelings are in harmony with the concrete collective anguish that surrounds him. His doubts and regrets are joined to the doubts and regrets of all those not participating in the overseas adventure, but who, staying behind in Portugal, will suffer the consequences of the voyage in their daily lives. Indecision, an anti-heroic trait par excellence, informs both da Gama's subjective existence and the objective insecurity of the journey.

Em tão longo caminho e duvidoso
Por perdidos as gentes nos julgavam,
As mulheres c'um choro piadoso,
Os homens com suspiros que arrancavam.
Mães, Esposas, Irmãs, que o temeroso
Amor mais desconfia, acresentavam
A desesperação e o frio medo
De já nos não tornar a ver tão cedo. (IV, 89)

[The people considered us already lost
On so long and uncertain a journey,
The women with piteous wailing,
The men with agonizing sighs;
Mothers, sweethearts, and sisters, made
Fretful by their love, heightened
The desolation and the arctic fear
We should not return for many a long year.]

There is a clear opposition to be observed between the certainty and expressions of confidence D. Manuel's dream inspired in the royal counselors, and the emphasis placed here on the word *dúvida* (doubt) and its adjective *duvidoso* (doubtful, uncertain, dubious), which appear three times over a short stretch of five stanzas:

Cheio dentro de dúvida e receio (IV, 87);
Em tão longo caminho e duvidoso (IV, 89);
Como, por um caminho duvidoso (IV, 91).

[Tormented by so many doubts and fears;
On so long and uncertain a journey;
Why, for so dubious a voyage.]

The idea of doubt gives effective expression to the uncertainty of all voyages whose protagonists give themselves over to chance.

The women intone the most pathetic strains of the chorus sung to the sailors upon their departure. The mothers' voices utter the mournful sobs of those who fear the death of their children at sea, with "bloated fish your only burial" (*onde sejas de peixes mantimento*). The wives' voices sharply and passionately deny, in the name of "us," their husbands' right to make the journey:

Por que is aventurar ao mar iroso
Esta vida que é minha e não é vossa?
Como, por um caminho duvidoso,
Vos esquece a afeição tão doce nossa?
Nosso amor, nosso vão contentamento,
Quereis que com as velas leve o vento? (IV, 91)

[Why do you risk on the angry seas
That which belongs to me, not you?
Why, for so dubious a voyage, do you
Forget our so sweet affection?
Is our passion, our happiness so frail
As to scatter in the wind swelling the sail?]

Is this epic, lyrical, dramatic? Epic is the choral historicity that serves as background staging for the expression of feelings, as well as the journey through the angry seas, the shadowy, risk-laden path of the explorers, and the wind that blows the Portuguese ships whichever way it pleases. Lyrical is the voice of the eternal feminine, which remains sweet even as it makes the bitterest complaints (the most moving among them that which invokes the idea of forgetting: "Why [...] do you/ Forget our so sweet affection?"). Also lyrical are love, frail happiness, and the intuition that the waves of the sea can undo fragile human ties in an instant. Finally, dramatic is the woman's interpellation of the man, her silent interlocutor caught between the contrary passions of love and glory. Dramatic is also the conflict to be seen within these divided families, as well as the deepening division between the ways in which those who depart and those who stay behind interpret existence. The text as a whole is epic, lyrical and dramatic—truly *poetic*—in its overcoming of rhetorical boundaries and its relativizing of individual genres, each of which, after all, uses multiple strategies to describe human relationships and appeal to the emotions in a variety of affective tones.

The chorus attains cosmic dimensions when the mountains echo in response the voices of the women, the elderly, and the children.

But the anticlimax is still to come. Collective lamentation is not enough: as a classical poet, Camões must present us with a whole, eloquent discourse in which he expresses truth in an irrefutable succession of reasoned arguments. Camões will excavate this *logos*, which runs counter to the voyage as a manifestation of national glory, from the repressed history of Portugal, the history of its people, and will present it in the speech of the *Velho do Restelo* (the Old Man of Restelo).

The Old Man, one of the many spectators on the shore, a man of the people speaking from "among the people," reject unequivocally the maritime undertaking at the exact moment of the ship's departure.[xvii] Point by point, his speech undermines the organic purpose of *Os Lusíadas,* which is to glorify da Gama's deeds, as well as the Aviz dynasty, Portugal's noble warriors, and the country's mercantile machine involved in the project. The Old Man leaves nothing untouched. He calls the noble motivating force of Fame, a much-invoked Renaissance topos, by its true name—the will to power: "Ó glória de mandar, ó vã cobiça / desta vaidade, a quem chamamos Fama!" ["O pride of power! O futile lust / For that vanity known as fame!"] (IV, 95). The feudal valorization of honor, still very much alive in the sixteenth century, is demystified as a "hollow conceit which puffs itself up / And which popular cant calls honour," and the Old Man launches an exemplary attack on the demagoguery the powerful employ in order to excite popular fanaticism to support the war machine: "They call distinction, they call honour / What deserves ridicule and contempt" [in the original, "Nomes com que se o povo néscio engana," names with which ignorant people are deceived)] (IV, 96). He sarcastically asks:

A que novos desastres determinas
De levar estes Reinos e esta gente?
Que perigos, que mortes lhe destinas,
Debaixo dalgum nome preeminente?
Que promessas de reinos e de minas
De ouro, que lhe farás tão facilmente?
Que famas lhe prometerás? Que histórias?
Que triunfos? Que palmas? Que vitórias? (IV, 97)

[To what new catastrophes do you plan

To drag this kingdom and these people?
What perils, what deaths have you in store
Under what magniloquent title?
What visions of kingdoms and gold-mines
Will you guide them to infallibly?
What fame do you promise them? What stories?
What conquests and processions? What glories?]

The voyage and all that it entails are presented as a disaster for Portuguese society, leading to a depopulated countryside, humiliating poverty and begging, the dispersal and death of able-bodied men, and ever-present adultery and the orphaning of the young. As Sá de Miranda had written before the publication of *Os Lusíadas,* "The kingdom disperses/ at the smell of this cinnamon" ("Ao cheiro desta canela / o reino se despovoa").[24]

The radical shift in the poem's perspective, from da Gama to the Old Man, gives us an idea of the spiritual force of a Camões who is both ideological and counter-ideological, a contradictory, living writer. His Old Man moves from condemnation to malediction, the final outcry of an impotent soul that refuses surrender. He categorically damns ambition, which since the collapse of the peace that reigned in Eden or in the Golden Age has consigned humanity to an iron age of labor and war. He casts a harsh light on the mythical figures of Prometheus, Daedalus, and Icarus, civilizing heroes of ancient Greece, to reveal them as victims of pride and *hybris.* Finally, he goes as far as to denounce progress and technical knowledge, implying that all Titanic adventures end in the ruin of their protagonists. The *nau* (ship) and *fogo* (fire), great inventions of a remote past that are about to guarantee the success of the colonial enterprise, are presented as signs of a grievous fate:

Oh! Maldito o primeiro que, no mundo,
Nas ondas vela pôs em seco lenho!
Digno da eterna pena do Profundo,
Se é justa a justa Lei que sigo e tenho!
....

Trouxe o filho de Jápeto do Céu
O fogo que ajuntou ao peito humano,

Fogo que o mundo em armas acendeu
Em mortes, em desonras (grande engano!)
Quanto melhor nos fora, Prometeu,
E quanto para o mundo menos dano,
Que a tua estátua ilustre não tivera
Fogos de altos desejos que a movera! (IV, 102-3)

[The devil take the man who first put
Dry wood on the waves with a sail!
Hell's fires are too good for him
If the laws I live by are righteous!
....

Prometheus stole the fire from heaven
Which rages in every human heart,
Setting the world ablaze with arms,
With death and dishonour, and all for nothing!
How much better for us, Prometheus,
How much less harmful for the world,
Had you not breathed into your famous statue
The restlessness that goads mankind to match you!]

At the outset of Portugal's maritime and colonial adventure, the enterprise's greatest writer voices a perplexed conscience: "What miserable luck! What a strange condition!" (IV, 104). This somber moment quickly passes, however, at least on the poem's factual surface. The navigators absorb the Old Man's harsh words, though they continue nonetheless, since *navegar é preciso*.[25]

Estas sentenças tais o velho honrado
Vociferando estava, quando abrimos
As asas ao sereno e sossegado
Vento, e do porto amado nos partimos.
E, como é já no mar costume usado,
A vela desfraldando, o céu ferimos,
Dizendo "Boa viagem!" Logo o vento
Nos troncos fez o usado movimento. (V, 1)

[As the honourable old man was uttering
These words, we spread our wings
To the serene and tranquil breezes
And departed from the loved harbour;
And, as is now the custom at sea,
The sails unfurled, we bellowed:
'God speed!', and the north winds as usual
Heard and responded, shifting the great hull.]

D. Manuel's allegorical dream has cleared the way, in tactical terms, for the conquerors' voyage: India's sacred rivers would flow to a sea dominated by the Portuguese. Those who stay behind tearfully denounce the brutality of events and, through the figure of the Old Man, recall the myths of humankind's youth, casting a negative light on the heroes who worked in the interest of material progress. But history moves forward, "shifting the great hull," and its winners and losers continue to confront one another.[xviii]

67

V. Beyond the Pale of Writing

The Old Man of Restelo and the populace who witnessed Vasco da Gama's departure were probably to become those migrants who, a half-century later, destitute and uprooted, would seek out land and work in India, Africa, and Brazil—though by this time they would no longer find a poet of Camões's stature to hear their voices and transmit them onto the page.

Since the sixteenth century, a culture has come into formation beyond the pale of writing, and in the context of a poor and oppressed people. Its language, the product of a diversity of racial and ethnic encounters, became as miscegenated as its speakers, such that today it borders on an anachronism to speak of a purely black, indigenous, or even rustic culture.

In the first years of colonization, the degree of ethnic difference was naturally quite high. The chroniclers of the sixteenth century, writers like Jean de Léry, Hans Staden, and Fernão Cardim, were still able to witness the ceremonies of the Tupi inhabitants of coastal Brazil.[26] And the rituals of Bahia's Afro-Brazilian population, which received scholarly documentation in the nineteenth century, had clearly originated in earlier centuries. In time, however, cultural symbiosis, whether *caboclo, mulato,* or *cafuzo* (i.e., indigenous-white, black-white, or indigenous-black), would come to dominate all aspects of symbolic and material production: cuisine, clothing, domestic life, speech, prayer, festivals, and so on. Without a doubt, acculturation is the paradigmatic theme of colonial anthropology.

Here we should make a preliminary conceptual distinction between markedly primitive or archaic expressions, that is, forms of material and spiritual culture peculiar to those who have always lived beyond the pale of writing, and *frontier expressions* that are the products of contact between popular culture and the erudite conventions introduced throughout the process of colonization. There is an evident difference between a cannibalistic ceremony witnessed by Staden while he was a captive of the Tupinambás, and the representation of war as it appears in a play written by Anchieta in Tupi and performed by the same Tupinambás, now exposed to Christianity and possibly even taught the Roman alphabet. To cite another contrasting pair, a religious rite performed by African slaves at the beginning of the eighteenth century, and described as *calundu,* in horrified terms, by Nuno Marques Pereira in his *Peregrino da América* (American Pilgrim), is not the same as a funeral procession led by the Confraternity of Our Lady of the Rosary of the Black Men of Vila Rica a few short years later.[27] Once more, the image of Exu (a Yoruba deity) or a geometric form designed by a Guarani weaver are not equivalent to a religious image created by a mulatto *santeiro* (a carver of saints), modeled on Portuguese sacred art and destined to be placed in a plantation chapel. And finally, the refrain sung in a *candomblé* ceremony among the *nagô* (Yoruba-origin) population of Salvador is far from identical to the hymn sung to the Virgin by the members of the Brotherhood of São José of the Black Men in a rural town somewhere in Minas Gerais.

All these, however, may be termed popular creations, with equal legitimacy and without regard to their ethnic affiliations and remote origins, precisely because origin does not determine. What is certain is that it was the poor who transmitted and sometimes were the direct producers of these expressions, whether *primitive* or *frontier, pure* or *mixed,* whether prohibited, tolerated, or actively promoted. They have equal anthropological value. It is the role of formal analysis to determine the stylistic components (or *traces,* as they are often termed) of these rites, narratives, and figures; and it is the task of sociohistorical interpretation to locate the meanings and values around which these symbolic creations are organized.

The majority of the expressions of non-literary culture can be described as complexes of signifying forms grounded in religious cult and devotion, and as institutions ordered so that through them the community may articulate its sense of existence and identity.

All that is necessary necessarily returns.

The repetition of formulas, the reiteration of rhythms, the abstract markings of Amerindian design, the fixed expressiveness retained in African masks, the rituals that are performed identically each time and everywhere, the precisely regular parts played by the participants in a chorus or dance: all of these reflect a desire to summon—by means of a reduced number of formulas, each pregnant with meaning—a simultaneously feared and adored transcendence (of the dead, of the gods, of the Other) that holds the personal and group destiny in its hand.

Nonetheless, as the process of acculturation continues and new influences are received from the colonizing matrix, a will toward stylization (already affected by erudite culture) emerges from the religious-popular base that gave rise to these expressions. The distinct Baroque style of seventeenth-century Minas Gerais (the *barroco mineiro*) is lighter and more stylized than the religious architecture of sixteenth-century Bahia. This is due to the veritable urban recolonization of Minas that brought wave upon wave of Portuguese settlers to the recently discovered gold-producing zone. The *mineiro* style seems late or anachronistic when compared in linear terms to European artistic development; however, the *barroco mineiro* was not an art produced by simple imitation or an offshoot of a displaced and derivative culture, but rather the result of an original merger of new, internal expressive needs with the still prestigious artistic models imported from Portugal and Italy.

In this frontier art form, the lived emotions of daily life in the colony— veneration, fear, love—are communicated through an economy of forms that, though they originated in remote spaces and times, are nonetheless flexible and capable enough to create strong, coherent images. The *mestiço* sensibility of colonial urban life and the models of sixteenth- and seventeenth-century Portuguese art converge in the figures carved by Aleijadinho through a synthesis in which the *high* style manifestly plays the orchestrating role. Yet what is important here is not the mathematical sum of the verifiable stylistic factors (so much of the cult, so much of the popular), but the need to determine, in each case, the perspective and meaning of the forms employed.

The relation between intervening forces is inverted once we take into consideration, for example, anonymous religious images, Carnaval street songs or dances, processional hymns, or orally transmitted narratives from the Iberian romance storytelling tradition. In all these frontier expressions, colonial popular inspiration manipulated, in its own way, materials of remotely European and lettered origin.

71

VI. A Caboclo Prayer in Greater São Paulo

I wish to recall, in this context, a religious ceremony I attended on the night of Saint Anthony in 1975, during a celebration dedicated to the saint. The small chapel, which still stands, is located about a hundred meters from the Raposo Tavares highway, near where it rises from Vargem Grande. Or, more exactly, it is located in Vila Camargo, in the yard of Nhá-Leonor's house. Neither the physical appearance of the neighborhood nor the occupations of its inhabitants justify referring to it as rural. No one plants crops, whether to eat or to sell, and everyone works in the city or in the construction sites on its outskirts. For many years now they have been working for wages, shopping in supermarkets, and watching television.

On that day, Nhá-Leonor had a barbeque and we ate beef from a freshly slaughtered animal (she had a cow killed once a year to fulfill a promise made to the saint). At ten the chaplain arrived. He was not a priest (the hostess had fallen out some time earlier with the Irish priests from Cotia, who were too modern for her taste), but a round man in his fifties with a pink face and smiling eyes who arrived from São Roque with two boys and a thin, middle-aged black woman.

The chaplain and his acolytes stood before the small blue altar adorned with stars made of glitter and began praying the rosary in a loud, strong voice. The faithful, almost all mulatto men who were drunk and stumbling back and forth, as well as some women, less poorly dressed than the men, responded to the prayer in equal tone and volume. This simple, pretty routine continued until all the Hail Marys and Pater Nosters were completed. A song to the Virgin Mary followed, with the chaplain intoning the hymn in Latin ("Salve Regina, mater misericordiae"); to my surprise, the congregation joined in immediately and without hesitation. And then came the truly astonishing moment for me: the recital of the entire long litany to Our Lady, also in Latin. I could not believe what I was witnessing: the same neighborhood *caboclos* whom I had seen slaving away every day as lowly

construction workers were putting a beautiful *caipira* spin on the medieval call-and-response prayer:[28]

"Espéco justiça - ora pro nobis
(Speculum justitiae)
"Sedi sapiença" - ora pro nobis
(Sedes sapientiae)
"Rosa mistia" - ora pro nobis
(Rosa mística)
"Domus aura" - ora pro nobis
(Domus aurea)
....

Mirror of justice, seat of wisdom, mystical rose, house of gold, morning
star, ark of the covenant, refuge of sinners, comforter of the afflicted,
queen of angels, queen of prophets, queen of peace—singing in his deep
voice, the chaplain enumerated all the attributes ascribed to the motherly
figure of Mary by the faithful down through the centuries. The tall black
woman followed him, improvising a melody on a *caipira* guitar and com-
plementing the music with at once ecstatic and controlled gestures of ado-
ration. And the boys and the congregation added a chorus of astounding
beauty.

After leaving the chapel I asked the chaplain about who had appren-
ticed him in his role. He responded that it was his father, who served as a
chaplain in the small rural landholdings of Sorocaba and Araçariguama.
The night was cool, the moon shone high above, but the freight-moving
trucks were still running heavily over the nearby asphalt.

***

What should we think of this fusion of the medieval Latin liturgy with
caipira intonation and musical accompaniment, and of its resistance to the
Catholic Church's dogged insistence since Vatican II, that the vernacular
be used in all religious celebrations?

The existence of this uniquely anachronistic chaplain says a good deal
about the autonomy of popular religious practice in relation to official

Church hierarchy. The old synthesis of Luso-colonial and rustic practices seems to have retained its inner dynamism in the ceremonies of these *caipiras,* quite urbanized in economic and quotidian terms. They passively resist the innovations promoted by the ecclesiastical establishment, which in recent decades has turned to an openly politicized pastoral language, and which during the 1970s and 80s joined in the opposition to the dominant political regime.[29]

Religious devotion, perhaps more than any other aspect of social life, is conducive to manifestations of symbolic persistence, which at some critical moments of reaction to the despotism of the modernizing state, take shape as an obstinate re-archaization of the community. This was the case with certain millenarian movements, like Canudos and the Contestado,[30] which were both regressive and prophetic, traditionalist and rebellious.[xix]

All seems to indicate that the colonial encounters of conquering, lettered cultures and conquered, non-lettered cultures represent a coexistence of extremes, with Western capitalism's most aggressive projects situating themselves among ancient, and in certain aspects resistant, patterns of life. New fieldwork and textual analyses must confirm the hypothesis that this cohabitation of the archaic with the modernizing does not represent a circumstantial paradox, but rather a recurrent feature of the history of colonization.

If we make a synchronic incision through those moments from the history of popular culture in which the force of colonization renews itself, we will find cases in which the new interrupts or disorders the old and the primitive, or in which the antiquated adopts, with barely a sign of distress, a few traces of the modern wherever traditional culture has put down roots and remains capable of surviving.

Oswaldo Elias Xidieh, one of the most perceptive scholars of Brazilian folklore, makes the following theoretical proposition: where there is a people, that is, where there is reasonably articulated and stable (or rooted, as Simone Weil would say) popular life, there will always be a traditional material and symbolic culture with a minimum of spontaneity, coherence, and a feeling for (if not awareness of) its identity. In its own way and within certain limits, this basically oral culture will absorb ideas and values from other sectors of society, be it, since colonial times, through the Church and the State, be it through schooling, propaganda, and the multiple institutions of the culture industry. This absorption does not imply,

75

however, a definitive self-destruction of popular culture, as the tradition-alists fear and the modernizers hope: it merely allows for a change in the appearance of certain objects and symbols.[xx]

There is no doubt that in situations of social trauma and forced migra-tion, the agents of popular culture suffer great material and spiritual shocks, and are only able to stay afloat if they attach themselves to the life raft of certain dominant economic structures. However, this sort of sur-vival does not (and cannot) have positive results in terms of cultural cre-ation, since it follows blindly the system's exploitative mandate. The migrant who reaches the city or a foreign land is a mutilated, deprived being. Fabiano, the protagonist of Graciliano Ramos's novel *Vidas Secas* (Barren Lives) is not a mythological figure invented by the author.[31] His conduct will oscillate between the most humiliated subservience and flashes of violence until, one day, his working conditions or the circum-stances of his community or family allow for the reconstruction of that web of signs and practices known as "popular culture." Every instance of relief or improvement will seem to him a product of fortune. And he will still almost always turns to cult, to religious faith of the type now found in the *seitas* (sects)—the collective term for the evangelical (normally Pentecostal and millenarian) churches that have proliferated in Brazil since the 1960s—as the weaver capable of spinning together the strands of his fate. If you live for a while in a poor neighborhood on the outskirts of São Paulo, Rio de Janeiro, Buenos Aires, or Lima, you will see the results of the migrant's peculiar condition. The migrant is not any more the figure of folklore, but neither is he fully absorbed into the culture industry that produces infinitely more than the people are capable of consuming. Capitalism has always both uprooted and reused (and only to the precise extent of its interests) the labor of migrants from traditional or marginal areas. And from what source do they derive the energy to lift themselves, albeit on rare occasions, a small step above the hard floor of necessity? In the majority of cases, it is only from that *heart of a heartless* world which gives form to beliefs and rituals, to words and songs, to prayer and trance, and which only communitary devotion is able to express.

VII. The Meaning of Forms in Popular Art

To return to a question posed by colonization, that of cultural encounter, we may observe that it is not always easy to determine precisely where the erudite ends and the popular begins in frontier symbolic forms.

In an anonymously carved religious image, for example, the piece's remote stylistic model may reside in the late Gothic period or in the Iberian Baroque, but the intense, concentrated and fixed, almost mask-like expressiveness of the face betrays an archaic-popular way of sculpting human soul in wood or clay. As Leonardo da Vinci advised: "Learn the secrets of expressive gestures from the deaf."

It would not be sufficient if, in the search for formal constants, we were to state that redundancy is an intrinsic feature of popular art. In fact, popular artistic expression plays host to numerous recurring marks, lines, colors, dance steps, rhythms, melodic phrases and hooks, echoes, refrains and entire verses, and opening and closing motifs. When we look through the traditional ballads and poems collected by Sílvio Romero in his *Cantos populares do Brasil* (Popular Songs of Brazil) and by Amadeu Amaral in his *Tradições populares* (Popular Traditions), the presence of repetition is more than apparent.[32] I cannot help quoting one of many possible examples, a children's rhyme that has been recited in northeastern Brazil since the beginning of the nineteenth century:

Amanhã é domingo,
pé de cachimbo,
Galo monteiro
Pisou na areia;
A areia é fina
Que dá no sino;
O sino é de ouro
Que dá no besouro;

O besouro é de prata
Que dá na mata;
A mata é valente
Que dá no tenente;
O tenente é mofino,
Que dá no menino;
Menino é valente
Que dá em toda gente.

[Tomorrow is Sunday,
a pipe's foot,
A mountain rooster
Stepped on the sand;
The sand is fine
It hits the bell;
The bell is gold
It hits the beetle;
The beetle is silver
It hits the forest;
The forest is brave
It hits the sergeant;
The sergeant's a sad sack,
He hits the boy;
The boy is brave
He hits all of us.][xxi]

The sound repetition we note in the pairings *domingo-cachimbo* and *monteiro-areia* is established from the first couplet, with rhymes and medieval *leixa-pren* intermingling.[33] Sound and meaning go hand in hand until the appearance of the choral image in which the smallest element of the piece, the boy, because he is brave, hits all of us. The boy closes the circle opened by another sign of smallness: the fine grains of sand, which hit the bell. The need for repetition is so great that the rhyme's global meaning ends up absorbing arbitrary internal couplings (the bell that hits the beetle, the brave forest, etc.) in the interest of preserving sonic and syntactic reiteration.

As is well known, repetition is present in high art as well, though there it is a concealed feature due to the requirements of the modernizing ideology inaugurated by the Romantic revolution, which valued the originality of a creative subject liberated from strict formal constraints. At times literary analysis does not progress beyond the task of identifying a text's recurrent and non-recurrent elements, its symmetrical and asymmetrical features, etc. It is up to interpretation to locate the cultural meaning of an expressive movement and to determine what perspective an artist reveals and what values he or she espouses when repeating a trace or a word.

The social explanation for repetition may be a community's desire to preserve collective harmony on the basis of a shared set of emotions and ideas. Repetition's psychological weight comes from memory, which more easily recalls symmetrical or at least recurrent elements.

Think of the consistency with which the figure of Christ, or *Bom Jesus* (Good Jesus), is represented in Luso-Brazilian religious imagery. He is and is not a human being like us. There is an austerity in his features, whether we refer to the examples found in Iguape, Pirapora, or Perdões, and his position is invariably frontal, severe and dignified. But within the confines of this hieratic posture, proper of a God, the passion has marked the body of Jesus, the Christ of the *Ecce Homo*. His arms are limp, his hands tied, his forehead cut by thorns, his eyes are hollow, and he is marked by the five wounds: he is a creature given over to destiny's fury. His scepter, which in Brazil may be made of sugar cane (some call him *Bom Jesus da Cana Verde*, Good Jesus of the Green Cane), is the sign of degraded, ridiculed royalty.

In this case, to reproduce always the same set of features of face and body is to conform to internal needs of social perception. The Good Jesus, the man who can pardon us because he is divine, the deity that suffers because he is human, must always appear identical to himself, to the artist who sculpts him, and to the devotee who contemplates and venerates him.

While the material used (wood, plaster, and most recently cardboard), the size and the execution may vary, reflecting differences in time period and technique, this in no way alters the image, which is reproduced in the name of its religious identity. It is identity that commands reiteration, in the first instance, and not vice versa. The saints represented in the *paulistinhas*, fired clay pieces that have been produced in São Paulo since the eighteenth century, are recognizable by certain invariable features or objects: Saint Benedict is identified by his dark beard and by the snake

79

coiled around his cassock; Saint Gertrude, by the heart of Jesus inscribed on her chest; Saint Joseph, by his boots, book, and lyre; Saint Gonçalo of Amarante, by a *caipira* guitar or book; and Saint Anthony, by his Franciscan habit and the Child Jesus in his arms.[xxii]

The repetition of certain features serves to reinforce the image's basic expressive aim. Sometimes it only takes one repeated element to identify the deity: this is the case of an image of the Child Jesus from Pernambuco, which Luís Saia recognized as Xangô (the Afro-Brazilian lord of storms and thunder), due to the red stripe painted across his stomach by followers of *candomblé*.[34] This sign, motivated though non-figurative, expressive and abstract, encompassing both color and trace, half-symbol and half-index, told the faithful that the figure, while not appearing as such to all, *was in fact Xangô*.[xxiii] The figure's sacred character was guaranteed by a single distinctive feature, the color red that always accompanies representations of Xangô. That which returns signifies, and only returns because it signifies.

The *high* visual arts from the Renaissance through the neoclassical period likewise flee from the dangers of undifferentiation. But the artist's methods are others. The academic sculptor engages in the *rifinitura* of the material as much as possible, creating meticulous, unique surface features in pursuit of a desired individualization in form and detail. The sculptor's tools mold the marble to produce a realistic representation of folds, rendering even the fringe of a robe an iconic feature. It is true that urban European craftsmanship also took pleasure in such masterful detailing (I am thinking of certain eighteenth-century Neapolitan crèches, of which the Museum of Sacred Art in São Paulo has a superb example), but we must recognize this as a case of Mannerist and Baroque erudite styles subtly making their way into the semi-popular Catholic imagination, which in Italy was particularly cognizant of the techniques of high art.

What we should take from this discussion is an awareness of popular art's dual character in the context of the Brazilian colonial condition: on the one hand, the almost schematic rigidity of general composition, which leads many to contrast archaic *abstraction* with the urban, cultured artist's figurative or realistic style; and, on the other hand, a form of expressiveness that is ontological rather than psychological. Rigidity and expressiveness transform the anonymous sacred piece into a mysterious object, an enigma simultaneously rough and solemn.

In formal terms, hieratic style reproduces and preserves postures and lines. By its nature, what is solemn cannot vary; it tends toward a self-perpetuating Gestalt, the good form. This holds true for all artistic expression identified as typical, whether high or low, sublime or grotesque.

Within this rather spacious and flexible internal model, which in itself contains all the virtual potential of art, given that it fuses the abstract and the expressive, popular culture remains open to a host of influences and impulses not screened for color, class, or nationality. Moreover, popular culture does not discriminate based on historical time, a fact that is rich in consequences. The culture of the people is local by force of its environment, but in its humble dialectical movement it becomes practically universal: it rejects nothing on principle, assimilating and refashioning everything by necessity. The *cheganças* and *congos* that since the eighteenth century have depicted the battles between Christians and Moors during the time of Charlemagne are notable examples of popular synchronicity.[35] As for sacred imagery, detailed stylistic analyses have revealed Byzantine, Gothic, and Baroque elements in devotional pieces from eighteenth-century São Paulo (Etzel).

It is precisely this democratic syncretism that was sometimes lacking in the artistic styles favored by erudite culture, particularly when they were codified by closed and self-perpetuating institutions. Much of what appears to be unchanging in popular art, and is therefore described as *typical*, is actually the product of a subjectively lived faithfulness to good form; whereas academic artists were instructed, over many generations, in a kind of forced repetition that resulted in imitation for imitation's sake, in an *etichetta (piccola etica...)*, or, in other words, in the repetition of a formula merely because of its social and political prestige. It is one thing to spontaneously experience and dedicate oneself to a tradition; it is quite another to demonstrate one's familiarity with it in an affected, pedantic, and snobbish manner. In English institutions of centuries past, *snob*, short for *sine nobilitate* (without nobility), was applied to students of uncertain noble origin.

As for expressiveness, in archaic popular art it is customarily all-encompassing, whereas in high art details tend to multiply for their own sake, with the artist delighting in the sophistication of the copy in face of the model.

It is worth asking what is occurring in anonymous sacred imagery when a particular anatomical detail is isolated or enlarged. This is a case of the part signifying for the whole, as in the *ex-votos* found at the base of crosses erected in northeastern Brazil, which Luís Saia examined in his fine study: enlarged hands and feet, sculpted with great care, speak to the amount of grace conceded in the cure. Here the part does not stand for itself, as in Mannerism; rather, it is the individual's overall well-being that gives thanks in plastic form. The basic scheme at work remains one of total expressiveness.

The *ex-votos* placed at the base of *cruzeiros de acontecido* (literally "crosses of something that happened," erected at the sites of tragic deaths), which are at the same time representations of promises made to Catholic saints and sculptures of remote African origin, challenge the observer to confront the problem of different ages operating simultaneously.

During its colonial acculturation, at least two time periods were present in Brazilian popular art: the time of Christian catechization and the time of black religiosity. The catechism, temporally located between the late medieval and Baroque periods, is merely traditional, whereas African religiosity is manifestly archaic. Catholicism, a key component of Western history, has exchanged its visual signs with successive artistic styles of the West: hence the tendency of Catholic art to shift from the purely allegorical to realistic figuration, and its acceptance during the Renaissance of classical ideas of perspective and representation. In contrast, the Bantu or Sudanese ritual art brought to Brazil by African slaves did not undergo this process of stylistic *updating*, but preserved its symbolic and animist heritage. In a way, colonial acculturation managed to fuse these two artistic traditions in the popular sacred object: it shaped the Catholic *ethos* of the promise, as depicted in the *ex-voto*, into the archaic mold of the African mask.

While the catechization of the Brazilian people was not exactly an *illusion*, as Nina Rodrigues understood it, it was certainly incomplete, operating as it did within a complex religious system that was older and more diffuse than official Catholicism. The *ex-voto*, located between two universes, serves as an example of frontier cultural product. It may also be understood in terms of *formal acculturation* (Roger Bastide's expression) or, following Melville Herskovits, as the *reinterpretation* of one culture by another.

VIII. The Prophets and the Calundu

Art that operates beyond the pale of writing preserves in an unchanging form certain traditional patterns and seems to survive *outside of history*, or at least outside the rhythm of the ideological history of Western Europe, which in turn is faithfully reproduced in the mental life of dominant colonial classes.

In reality, frontier culture exhibits a certain permeability with regard to symbolic forms from other eras, however remote, which is indicative of a different historical consciousness: a broad, knowing synchrony that makes the most of its particular circumstances. "Aleijadinho's prophets are not Baroque, they are biblical," exclaimed Giuseppe Ungaretti after inspecting them during a 1968 trip to Minas Gerais with the photographer Sérgio Frederico.[36] Since a properly biblical statuary does not exist, what the poet saw with his eagle eye was the expression in stone of a religiosity more majestic and choral and, at the same time, more intrepid and freer than that allowed for by the Mannerist models of eighteenth-century sculpture.

The art of colonial Brazil could only be fully appreciated when bourgeois academic taste began its period of terminal decline at the end of the *belle époque*.[xxiv] The modernists, who were drawn both to the primitive and to the new in their desire to rediscover Brazil, redeemed the *barroco mineiro* from the disdainful evaluation it had received at the hands of the neoclassicists of the French Artistic Mission of 1816.[37] An enthusiastic historian celebrated the 1816 mission in the following terms:

> In architecture, colonial institutions, feelings and ideas upheld during the Baroque, the Jesuit, the Plateresque, and the Churrigueresque periods were replaced by neoclassical feelings and actions.
>
> In painting, the ancient world, mythology and history replaced the almost exclusively religious work of the *santeiro* artists of the Colony and of the last Viceroyalty. (qtd. in Taunay 51)

Note the twice reiterated idea of the *substitution* performed by the new artistic school that accompanied D. João VI to Brazil and replaced the religious and popular Baroque of the *santeiros* with the secular and modernizing neoclassical style. As is well known, much of our civil architecture, particularly in nineteenth-century Rio de Janeiro, conformed to neoclassical standards. Our so-called national painting would likewise follow French academic standards, beginning in the Regency period (1831-40) and to a greater extent during the Second Reign (1840-89).[38] Gonçalves de Magalhães, the *romântico arrependido* (regretful Romantic), and Araújo Porto Alegre were both disciples of Debret.[39] Thus it is not surprising that Bernardo Guimarães, a Romantic and a regionalist born and raised in Ouro Preto, wrote of Aleijadinho's statues of the prophets at Congonhas do Campo with a total lack of aesthetic understanding yet with awe at the artist's exceptional energy:[40]

> We know that these statues are the work of a sculptor with a missing or deformed right hand, who needed to attach his tools to his wrists in order to work.
>
> It is for this reason, no doubt, that his artistic execution is far from perfect. One need not be an expert to recognize the errors in design, the lack of harmony and proportion in certain forms. Deformed heads, inexact proportions, too-heavy and shortened bodies, and many other major and minor errors reveal these prophets to be the products of a rough, uninstructed chisel. That said, their postures are generally characteristic, imposing, and majestic, they are artfully assembled, and at times the uneducated sculptor's tools managed to give their faces expressions worthy of prophets.
>
> The sublime Isaiah, the terrible, somber Habakkuk, and the melancholy Jeremiah are especially notable for the beauty and solemnity of their expression and posture. If we do not look at them with the minute and scrutinizing eye of an artist, an initial glance is sure to result in a strong impression of respect and even wonder. These statues seem to be rough, incorrect copies of fine artistic models, which the artist had in front of him or imprinted on his imagination.[xxv]

What Bernardo Guimarães, with his Romantic sensibility, could not help but admire was precisely Aleijadinho's totalizing expressiveness: he writes of *the sublime, somber, melancholy, expressions worthy of prophets, beauty and solemnity of their expression, a strong impression of respect and even wonder.* Yet what Guimarães's academic criteria made him reject was the very artistic approach that granted the figures their expressive force. Aleijadinho's creative impulse prevented him from applying (nor did he need) correct anatomical proportion, the perspective of a Donatello, the virtuosity of mimetic detail or the sweet harmony of spiraling curves; his approach required other symbolic forms and strategies for execution. The last sentence of Guimarães's commentary, which takes for granted the existence of "fine artistic models" of which the sculptures in question are "rough, incorrect copies," betrays the aesthetic distortion of a gaze hardened by neoclassical formulas.

This seems to be a case of structurally inevitable misunderstanding. Learned aesthetic criteria have their own history, marked by European cultural battles: the opposition between the neoclassical standards of the Enlightenment and the devout, semi-popular Baroque "obscurantism," which is seen summarily as an obstacle to be overcome. When the spirit of this struggle makes its way into the ideology of the colonized country's ruling elite, it manifests itself in critical judgments against cultural expressions of other segments of society, not only those situated at the purely popular level but also on the frontier between the illiterate and the educated. In this way, elitism becomes an inescapable feature of Latin American ideological development, insofar as the general ideas of evolution, progress and civilization remain divorced from the values of social and cultural democracy.

Through the division of labor and power, official taste during the nineteenth and early twentieth centuries differentiated the values of the colonizer and the colonized, reducing the latter to non-values. As a result, the colonized always experienced their symbolic universe ambiguously, as both positive (in itself) and negative (for the external other and for the interiorized other in oneself).

One of the aims of this book is to suggest that the cultural schism that accompanied modernization as it was experienced by elites manifested itself in other ways, and with apparently harsher consequences, in the interior of the colonial context. It is well known that the first Jesuits in Brazil effectively demonized Tupi religious practices, with the exception of Tupã, arbitrarily identified with the God of the Bible. Non-acceptance was even more pronounced with regard to African rites.

The Prophet Ezekiel.

"Aleijadinho's prophets are not Baroque, they are biblical."
Giuseppe Ungaretti

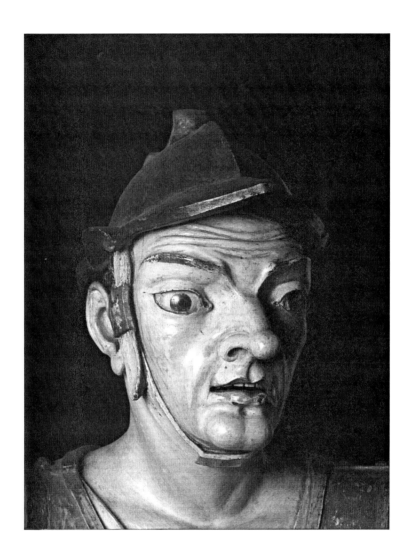

Roman soldier, Aleijadinho's workshop.

Caricatural figures of the Stations of the Cross: art at the frontier between the erudite and the popular.

Reading Nuno Marques Pereira's Baroque allegory *Compêndio narra-tivo do Peregrino da América* (The American Pilgrim's Narrative Compendium), published in 1718, I find an episode that illustrates how religious differences were resolved in pure and simple exorcism. The Pilgrim is staying in the house of a generous plantation owner. However, he cannot sleep at night because of the noises made by the slaves during their religious dances. Here is what happens next:

> He asked me how I had passed the night. I responded: "Comfortably, but awake. I couldn't fall asleep the whole night." Concerned, he asked me why. I told him that I had been tormented by the noise of *atabaques, pandeiros, canzás, botijas,* and *castanhetas*; the cacophony was so horrendous that it seemed like the very chaos of Hell [...] "Now I remember what I wanted to ask," I said to him. "What are *Calundus*?" "They're dances, divinations," he said to me, "that these blacks say are customary in their land, and which they perform here whenever they get together, in order to find out the causes of sicknesses they're suffering from, or where to find things they've lost, or to have good fortune in their hunts and in the harvest, and for many other purposes besides.

The landowner's explanation, which in fact serves as a good anthropo-logical lesson, describes in simple terms the integrating functions of a rit-ual that, transplanted from Africa, managed to survive in the harsh condi-tions of the fields and slave quarters.[xxvi] But the Pilgrim is neither convinced nor mellowed. On the contrary, he condemns his host's toler-ance to the point of calling both him and the slaves *excomungados* (ex-communicates) for violating the first commandment, for the sins of idola-try and devil worship, just as the poet Gregório de Matos had done a generation earlier in his condemnation of Afro-Bahian customs, written from the perspective of the city of Salvador da Bahia:

> Que de quilombos que tenho
> Com mestres superlativos,
> nos quais se ensina de noite
> os calundus e feitiços!
> ....
> O que sei é que em tais danças

Satanás anda metido,
e que só tal padre-mestre
pode ensinar tais delírios.

[I have quilombos
with great masters,
where at night they teach
calundus and spells!
....
What I know is that Satan
is involved in those dances,
for only this master priest
could teach such delirium.]

("Queixa-se a Bahia por seu bastante procurador,
confessando que as culpas, que lhe increpam, não
são suas, mas sim dos viciosos moradores que em
si alberga.")

[Bahia protests, through its advocate, that the faults
attributed to it are not its own, but those of the
wicked persons who find shelter in it.]

Meanwhile, in *Peregrino da América,* our inquisitorial Pilgrim moves
from words to action. He calls for the "Master of the *Calundus,*" probably
the *babalaô,* asks him what he does, and gives him a bizarre etymological
lecture in order to demonstrate the demonic character of his art:

"Tell me, son (who should more properly be called father of wickedness),
what are *Calundus*?" He responded with great reticence and shame that
they were a custom from his land, feasts of entertainment and divination.
"Don't you know," I asked him, "what the word *Calundus* means in
Portuguese? The black man told me he didn't. "Well I'd like to tell you," I
said, "what the etymology of the name means. In Portuguese and Latin, it
means this: they are both silent. *Calo duo.* Do you know who these two are
who keep silent? They are you and the devil. The devil keeps silent, and so
do you, about the great sin of the pact you've made with the devil, and which

you're teaching to the others, also making them sin, so that you'll take them with you to Hell when they die for what they did here in your company." (1: 123)

The landowner, the *pai-de-santo,* and the slaves were all terrified, and the Pilgrim asked them to

bring to him all the instruments they used in those diabolical dances. They did this and the instruments were brought to the *terreiro,* where a great bonfire was lit and they threw everything in. My clearest memory is of smelling the horrible stench and hearing the noises made by the *tabaques, botijas, canzás, castanhetas* and *pés de cabras.* There was smoke so black that no one could bear it. It had been a clear day, but it soon darkened with a fog so black that night seemed to be falling. So then I, who trusted entirely in His Divine Majesty, prayed the Creed, and right away a fresh gust of wind blew and everything dissipated.

This is followed by a long narrative, filled with other examples of idolatrous and libidinal dealings with the devil, acts in which many souls had been damned for all eternity.

What is most striking about this episode of the *Peregrino da América* is the war without mercy waged by official religion against the rites of African origin, a war that culminates in a true *auto-da-fé* in which the slaves' sacred instruments are destroyed. And it is worth noting how the Pilgrim removes the fetid cloud that blocks out the sun: he recites the Creed, just as someone might recite a magic spell against an enemy, "and just then a fresh gust of wind blew and everything dissipated."

In the process of colonial acculturation the more modern protagonist will at times regress to the arcane *ethos* of past eras.

We can extract a common and more general meaning from these (mis)encounters in the form of a dialectical complex composed of distinct social periods, whose simultaneity is structural, just as both the meeting together and the opposition of the dominating and the dominated are structural. The eye of the colonizer did not forgive, or barely tolerated, the articulation and survival of difference. The rigid orthodoxy enshrined by the Council of Trent was violently opposed to Afro-Brazilian dances and songs. Later, French-modeled academic taste would malign the archaic-popular style of the *barroco mineiro,* still alive in the religious architecture of the nineteenth century. Cultures (or cults) invariably draw on their dominant position in passing judgment on the cultures and cults of others. Colonization delays democratization also in the world of symbols.

In order to be received sympathetically, the symbolic formations of the colonized had to wait until the first quarter of the twentieth century, a period in which the European intelligentsia, then in the midst of a profoundly self-critical examination of Western imperialism, began reconsidering popular art, the American Baroque style, and African cultures. Franz Boas's anti-racist anthropology, which was brought to Brazil by Gilberto Freyre, the Parisian avant-garde in the visual arts and its valorization of *art nègre,* and shortly thereafter the reconsiderations of Baroque aesthetics by German and Spanish stylistics: these are some of the disparate critical strands that contributed to a new attitude among the intellectual elites of Latin America. While this sentiment might be confused in certain respects with the nationalism then surging through the ex-colonial nations, it transcended this framework of militant ideology as it turned to the universalizing potentialities of art and religion. Hence the propitious convergence of cosmopolitism and rooted localism in the avant-garde manifestations of those years of Latin American and Afro-Antillean renaissance.

Author's Notes

[i] Augusto Magne tells us that "*[c]olo* is derived from *Kwelo,* which means to move around something, to circulate. The meaning of the root is clearly illustrated by the second part of Greek compound masculine nouns like *bou-kólos* (cowherd), *ai-pólos* (goatherd), *amphí-pólos* (servant, he who moves around a cow, a goat, or the master of the house, and takes care of them). The idea of 'taking into one's care,' which is apparent in these terms, explains some of the applications of *colo* in Latin; its agrarian connotations are explained, on the other hand, by the rural character of the ruling class during Rome's earliest days. While in Greek *Kwel-* carries the meanings of 'to move' and 'to habitually find oneself in,' the Latin *col-* carries the specific meaning of 'to inhabit' or 'to cultivate'; compare how the aforementioned compound words convey the idea of 'occupying oneself with.' The ideas of habitation and cultivation are present from the earliest times because of the connection drawn between these ideas by the rural population."

[ii] In the *Lexicon totius latinitatis,* Aegidio Forcellini distinguishes, with lapidary definitions, between colony and municipality: "*Colonia* differt a *municipio:* municipes enim sunt cives alicuius municipii, legibus suis et suo jure utentes: coloni sunt cives unius civitatis in aliam deducti, et eius jure utentes, a qua sunt propagati" [A *colony* differs from a *municipality:* municipals in truth are citizens of a municipality, who live by their own laws and their own right; colonists are citizens of a city who are brought to another, and who live by the laws of the city from which they originated]. And he specifies one meaning of colony: "Colonia est pars civitatis, aut sociorum deducta in aliquem locum, colendi et inhabitandi gratia: itemque ipse locus" ["A colony is the part of a city (state) or society that has been displaced to another land in order to cultivate and inhabit it; 'colony' also refers to the place itself"] (692-3).

[iii] See Vitorino Magalhães Godinho's *Economia dos descobrimentos henri-quinos.*

[iv] On the ancientness of funerary rites, see Henri Gastaut's succinct but well founded "Alguns comentários a respeito do culto do crânio."

[v] In *Il materialismo storico,* passim.

[vi] Here I refer to the entire tradition of *progressive critique* of Max Scheler, Mannheim, Benjamin, Horkheimer, Adorno, Sartre, and Merleau-Ponty, which beginning in the 1920s called into question the certainties of the bourgeois thought of the Enlightenment, along with its positivist or evolutionist derivations.

[vii] Moore and Aveling's 1887 translation is the first English edition of *Capital*'s first volume. Ernest Untermann's translations of the second and third volumes were published in 1907 and 1909, respectively.

[viii] Manuel Galich quotes this account from *Argentina indígena, vísperas de la conquista* by Rex González y Pérez.

ix On Montaigne's knowledge of Las Casas, see Juan Durán Luzio, "Bartolomé de las Casas y M. de Montaigne: escritura y lectura del Nuevo Mundo." The theme of the *leyenda negra* has been ably taken up by Gustavo Gutiérrez in his *Dios o el oro en las Indias.*

x "Young nations are a vast expanse open to violent individual activities that in the metropolis would clash with certain prejudices, with a prudent and regulated view of life. However, in the colonies they can be developed more freely and can as a consequence better affirm their value. In this way colonies may to a certain extent serve as safety valves for modern society. This would be of immense value, even if it were the only benefit of colonization" (qtd in Césaire 20).

xi Raymundo Faoro offers an excellent analysis of the linked themes of centralization and the authoritarian tradition in Brazil in his *Os donos do poder: Formação do patronato político brasileiro.*

xii Caio Prado Jr., *Formação do Brasil contemporâneo;* Nelson Werneck Sodré, *Formação da sociedade brasileira;* Celso Furtado, *Formação econômica do Brasil;* Fernando Novais, *Portugal e Brasil na crise do antigo sistema colonial;* Jacob Gorender, *O escravismo colonial;* Maria Sylvia Carvalho Franco, "Organização social do trabalho no período colonial."

xiii The author's broader thesis rests on the assumption that "the Portuguese, in their ability to adapt themself to all environments, many of which ran counter to their own racial and cultural characteristics, revealed a greater colonizing capacity than the other [European] peoples, perhaps more closely tied to the peculiar conditions of the Old World" (188).

xiv See Eduardo Hoornaert, "Rio de Janeiro, uma igreja perseguida" and Américo Jacobina Lacombe, "A Igreja no Brasil colonial." On the situation in Bahia, see Thales de Azevedo's exemplary study *Igreja e Estado em tensão e crise.*

xv Vico wrote the following: "In children memory is most vigorous, and imagination is therefore excessively vivid, for imagination is nothing but extended or compounded memory" (75). This translation follows the 1744 edition of Vico's text (Book I, Section II, Paragraph L).

xvi The article "Colonisation" in the 1928 edition of Larousse encyclopedia (which remains virtually unchanged since the encyclopedia's nineteenth-century edition) reads as follows: "L'histoire nous montre tous les peuples supérieurs en civilisation fondant des colonies, mûs par une force instinctive et parfois malgré eux." [History shows us that all peoples who are superior in civilization are moved by an instinctive force and sometimes in spite of themselves to found colonies.] (2: 351)

xvii Why did the poet choose an anonymous old man, someone of whom we know nothing other than his advanced age and his "venerable appearance," as the poem's spokesman of discontent? The weight of the Old Man's experience was certainly a strong factor in this choice, as was, moreover, the uniqueness of this very experience. The little we know of the Portuguese demographics of the time leads us to believe that the average life expectancy could not have been more than forty years. Vasco da Gama was not yet thirty when D. Manuel appointed him to lead his fleet to India, and Pedro Álvares Cabral was only thirty-two when he reached the Brazilian coast. The youth of those who crewed the Portuguese ships can easily be guessed. In this context, old age conveys a kind of uncommon wisdom, as well as prudence and a groundedness that stands in contrast to the daring of the youthful sailors.

xviii In *A literatura portuguesa e a expansão ultramarina,* Hernâni Cidade writes of what he calls expressively the "shadows in the painting," assembling various literary and historical episodes that communicate sadness, anguish, and even open indignation at the dark side of Portugal's overseas enterprise. Among the "chords in the great elegy" are passages from Garcia de Resende's *Cancioneiro geral,* João de Barros's *Décadas,* Diogo do Couto's *Soldado prático,* and later the tormented *História trágico-marítima,* whose twelve shipwreck narratives provide effective testimony of the disasters suffered by the Portuguese in the Atlantic and Indian oceans. Camões was well aware of the sinister side of the expansionist adventure: the lies, raids, killings (some of which involved attempted cannibalism by starved Portuguese shipwreck victims), rapes, escapes, and suicides provided him with ample material for an anti-epic of colonization.

xix See the following exemplary studies: Maria Isaura Pereira de Queiroz's *O messianismo no Brasil e no mundo;* Maurício Vinhas de Queiroz's *Messianismo e conflito*; and Duglas Teixeira Monteiro's *Os errantes do novo século.* Behind all of them is Euclides da Cunha's classic *Os Sertões* (1902).

xx See Xidieh's *Narrativas pias populares* (1967) and *Semana santa cabocla* (1972), both published by the Institute for Brazilian Studies, University of São Paulo. "Popular Culture," states Xidieh, "is a historical phenomenon, but whose date of origin can only be sociologically or anthropologically established through identification of situations in which old and new socio-cultural models enter into conflict. By the time history 'speaks,' it has already occurred [...] Yet what I want to underscore is that popular culture, while it is no longer primitive culture, nonetheless perpetuates, through inheritance or discovery, innumerable of its traces and patterns: *tradition, analogy, consideration of the natural world's laws, a magical approach to life, a sense of repetition.* But its dynamic can also be expressed through a popular saying, 'God makes things better hour by hour' (*De hora em hora Deus melhora*), which demonstrates its capacity for renovation and re-elaboration" ("Cultura popular" 14).

xxi See also João Ribeiro's commentary in *O folclore,* XXVII.

xxii See Eduardo Etzel, *Imagens religiosas de São Paulo.*

xxiii See Saia's *Escultura popular brasileira.*

xxiv Mário de Andrade wrote the very first essay dealing with Aleijadinho's artistic and social significance. His "O Aleijadinho" (1928), later included in *Aspectos das artes plásticas no Brasil,* deals particularly with the artist's sculptural expressiveness and his condition as a mulatto.

xxv Published in 1872 in *O seminarista.* For criticism of this point, see Lourival Gomes Machado's article "Muito longe da perfeição."

xxvi According to Pierre Verger, the term *candomblé* only came into use in Brazil in the first years of the nineteenth century or, more precisely, in 1826: "Before this time, the most common term used to describe the body of African-origin religious practices seems to have been *Calundu,* an Angolan word. Another term used was *batuque,* though this was used to describe both religious rituals and secular forms of entertainment" (227).

Editor's Notes

The following notes, intended for the non-specialist reader, are meant to clarify references that did not require greater explanation in Alfredo Bosi's original text. Readers familiar with Brazilian and Luso-Brazilian history and intellectual debates may, of course, ignore these explanations.

[1] The *leyenda negra* is a modern term that refers to the proliferation, beginning in the mid-sixteenth century, of stories about the atrocities committed by the Spanish *conquistadores* in America. The creation of the *leyenda negra* may be associated with the great debate regarding the spiritual and physical conquest of the Amerindians and the preponderant role of the Spanish crown in the conquest of America, both of which form the background of Bartolomé de las Casas' accounts mentioned by Bosi later in the text.

[2] The word "Tupi" refers both to the language that predominated along the coast where the Portuguese disembarked and broadly to the peoples that spoke this language.

[3] The name Sete Povos das Missões refers to an area that today comprises parts of southern Brazil, Paraguay, and Argentina. Here the Jesuits, beginning before the Treaty of Madrid (which in 1750 reestablished the boundaries between Portuguese and Spanish America), established an extensive network of settlements in which Amerindians were educated in the Catholic faith, according to Ignatian teachings. The Jesuits' pedagogical and economic influence extended throughout Brazil, and for almost the entire colonial period was in open conflict with local property holders, particularly in terms of the battle for control and tutelage of the Amerindians, who were used as slave laborers by Portuguese and Luso-Brazilian landowners. The *bandeirantes* were the explorers of the Brazilian backlands who engaged in private and official expeditions to the interior of the colony, seeking Amerindian captives, gold, and precious stones. These expeditions frequently departed from the Piratininga highlands, where the town of São Paulo (founded by the Jesuits in the mid-sixteenth century) was located. The *bandeirantes* were especially active during the seventeenth century, at which time they were in constant conflict with the Jesuits who sought to protect the Amerindians from the *paulistas,* as the *bandeirantes* were often termed. Traditional historiography and iconography have tended to idealize the figure of the *bandeirante,* projecting the image of an intrepid explorer-as-civilizing agent and frequently obscuring the extremely violent character of the *bandeirantes'* simultaneously economic and civilizational crusade. For information on the *bandeirantes* in English, see Richard Morse, ed., *The Bandeirantes: The Historical Role of the Brazilian Pathfinders.*

[4] Bosi refers here to the expansion of the agricultural frontier into sparsely pop-

ulated areas during the Brazilian dictatorship's repeated efforts at economic development during the 1970s and 80s. These efforts favored agribusiness (and the production of grains, especially soy) and exacerbated the struggle for land, creating
zones of conflict between the representatives of large-scale agricultural capital,
large- and medium-scale producers, and a dispossessed population composed of
mestiços and even Amerindians. From this context emerged important movements
that contested the regime and its economic model. These movements have survived
up to the present, placing agrarian reform at the center of the debate over agricultural and land policy in Brazil.

5 *Literatura de cordel,* whose name refers to the *corda,* or string, on which the
printed stories were originally hung, constitutes a bridge between the old Iberian
storytelling tradition and more recent popular narratives that, in the context of a
literate or semi-literate culture, deal with the most diverse political and social
problems of the day, as well as offer tales of a moral character. This is a popular
and plural literature with wide urban and rural circulation, which remains active
in today's Brazil. It is closely connected to the oral tradition of *cantadores* and
repentistas, the wandering troubadours of the Brazilian northeast. See, in English,
Candace Slater, *Stories on a String: The Brazilian "Literatura de Cordel."*

6 Gregório de Matos Guerra (1636-1696), born in Bahia and educated in
Coimbra, is the author of a poetry that described, in a satirical and moralizing vein,
the daily life of Bahia's upper and popular classes. Matos's verses, sometimes mystical, frequently erotic and almost always burlesque, possess a style and vivacity
that, according to Bosi himself, would not be "equaled in all of the history of later
Brazilian satire" (*História concisa* 40).

7 Gilberto Freyre's studies of Brazilian society are available in English: *The
Masters and the Slaves: A Study in the Development of Brazilian Civilization* and
The Mansions and the Shanties: The Making of Modern Brazil. Sérgio Buarque de
Holanda's essay "Monsoons" has been published in English in the aforementioned
volume edited by Richard Morse (*The Bandeirantes: The Historical Role of the
Brazilian Pathfinders*).

8 The *engenhos,* referred to here alongside their equivalents in Spanish
America (the Mexican and Peruvian *encomienda* and the *hacienda* of the Platine
region), are units of production that also functioned as political and social entities.
They had a high degree of autonomy during the colonial period, and furnished a
true model of sociability that would be amply considered by the Brazilian historiography discussed by Bosi in this book. The *quilombos* are, as has already been
mentioned, Afro-Brazilian maroon settlements, which the Portuguese crown and
Brazilian colonists would harshly combat. The most famous of the *quilombos* was
Palmares, which has been elevated to mythical status and remains a symbol of
resistance and of Afro-Brazilian identity. Palmares enjoyed enormous political
importance throughout the seventeenth century, until it was defeated by military
forces principally composed of *bandeirantes.*

9 The term *paulista* refers here to the fact that the *bandeirantes'* expeditions departed primarily from the São Paulo region. As has already been noted, the Jesuits and Amerindians identified the *paulistas* with the *bandeirantes,* their eternal enemies.

10 José de Anchieta (1534-1597), born in the Canary Islands, traveled to Brazil as a very young man and, with his fellow Jesuit Manoel da Nóbrega, founded the college of Piratininga around which the town of São Paulo would be built. Anchieta was a prolific writer (in Portuguese, Spanish, Latin, and Tupi) of plays, letters, and mystical poems in which the old motifs of the Iberian storytelling canon are coupled with the ascetic mindset of the Ignatians. While the latter does not entirely succeed in suppressing the lyricism of Anchieta's writings, they nevertheless bear clear witness to an overriding concern with conversion and the need to respect the liturgy—all in the context of their intensely allegorical character. It is worth noting how Bosi understands Anchieta as the first in a series of figures that embody the contradictions placed on the subject by his or her colonial condition: "The case of Anchieta seems exemplary because he is our first militant intellectual. The fact that throughout his life he was inspired by an apostle's undeniable good faith only makes more dramatic his response to the near-fatality that divides the colonizing man of letters between two codes: one for his own use (and that of his peers) and another to be used by the people. In the former there is an effusion of subjectivity; in the latter, an allegorical didacticism that is rigid and authoritarian. In the former there is the mysticism of *devotio moderna;* in the latter, the missions' morality of terror" (*Dialética* 93).

11 *Curumim* is the Tupi word for "boy."

12 "Tupã" is a Tupi word that refers to thunder as a cosmic entity, which the Jesuits linked in their work of symbolic translation and conversion to the God of Catholicism.

13 João Ramalho (1493?-1580) was a Portuguese colonizer who established himself among the Amerindians along what is now the coast of the state of São Paulo. A sort of *paulista* civilizing hero and a prolific agent of miscegenation who sold Brazil wood and indigenous slaves, Ramalho became a legendary figure, alternately revered and scorned by posterity. Many of Anchieta's letters refer to a period of war during the mid-sixteenth century between the Portuguese, French (who at the time were established in Rio de Janeiro), Jesuits, and various regional indigenous groups who were joined in what became known as the "Confederation of the Tamoios." During the nineteenth century, the confederation would be celebrated in a nativist and nationalist tone in the verses of the Romantic poet Gonçalves de Magalhães.

14 Father Antônio Vieira (1608-1697) is one of the greatest prose writers of the Portuguese language. He is especially noted for his many *Sermons,* which he used as the vehicle for his simultaneously political and religious ideas, and in which he discussed issues such as the condition of the Amerindians and blacks in the colony,

Portugal's power in the world, and modern and ancient readings of the Bible. Vieira's political audacity was matched by his literary daring, which gave his native idiom some of its greatest moments and inspired the poet Fernando Pessoa to call him the "Emperor of the Portuguese language." A Jesuit, Vieira was a valued ambassador of the Crown, charged with advancing imperial causes (for an Empire conceived as both temporal and eternal) throughout Europe. Nonetheless, he had serious problems with the Inquisition and was even jailed for his heterodox theses, which identified the biblical Fifth Empire with the Portuguese Empire.

[15] This is a reference to *O Guarani,* a historical novel by Brazilian Romanticism's principal writer, José de Alencar (1829-1877). The Marizes play a central role in the novel's plot, which crosses European Romantic motifs (particularly the idealization of a prior age free of the convulsions of modern times) with exotic elements offered to the author's imagination by the novel's tropical setting. In the novel, the heroine Cecília, the daughter of Dom Antônio de Mariz, marries the noble savage Peri, forming one of the most celebrated couples in Brazilian literature.

[16] Bosi refers to Joaquim Maria Machado de Assis (1839-1908), Brazil's most important writer and the author of such novels as *Memórias póstumas de Brás Cubas* and *Dom Casmurro.* Various of his novels and some short stories have been translated into English. Over the past few decades, a significant body of criticism on the author has developed in English. See, for example, the volume *The Author as Plagiarist: The Case of Machado de Assis* edited by João Cezar de Castro Rocha.

[17] The colonial poet José Basílio da Gama (1741-1795) was under the protection of the Portuguese plenipotentiary minister the Marquis of Pombal for a good portion of his career. His most celebrated and important poem, the epic *O Uraguai,* was published in 1769. In its elegant decasyllables, composed in blank verse, an idealization of the savage runs parallel to the exaltation of the Portuguese military forces. The poem narrates the expulsion of the Jesuits by the Portuguese and Spanish forces and the destruction of their missions in the region of the Sete Povos (see note 3 above). Bosi analyzed da Gama's poem in an important text ("As sombras das luzes na condição colonial") that was published after his *Dialética da colonização,* and in which the theme of resistance allows him to uncover, in the voice of the poet, a kind of popular epos that connects the Guarani massacred in the area of the missions to an entire lineage of sacrifice that includes the Inca and the Araucanian, in sum all "subjects" that cannot fully lift themselves up under the weight of the colonial system. See Bosi's *Literatura e resistência.*

[18] Antonio Francisco Lisboa (1738-1814), known as Aleijadinho (the Little Cripple), lived for practically his entire life in the Vila Rica region, where he was a prolific and celebrated sculptor. His religious images are a powerful demonstration of what a late Baroque genius is capable of when confronted with conditions that differ from those prevailing in Europe. Regarding the statuary of Minas Gerais, Myriam Andrade Ribeiro de Oliveira suggests that in it "a certain ingenuity frequently shows through and the robes [featured in the sculptures] do not always

hang in a logical manner." The nickname by which the sculptor is commonly known refers to the fact that at around forty years of age he acquired an illness (his biographers assume it was a venereal disease) that progressively limited his hand movement and caused him to lose his fingers. This required him to sculpt using tools attached to his wrists. The churches Aleijadinho adorned in and around Vila Rica (now Ouro Preto) in the region of Minas Gerais are important tourist destinations in Brazil. His best-known works are without a doubt the prophets sculpted in soapstone, as well as the "stations of the cross" that depict the passion of Jesus, in the Santuário do Bom Jesus de Matosinhos in Congonhas do Campo. For more on this topic, see the studies by Oliveira, Olinto Rodrigues dos Santos Filho, and Antonio Fernando Batista dos Santos in *O Aleijadinho e sua oficina: Catálogo das esculturas devocionais.* See also Claus Meyer, *Passos da Paixão: o Aleijadinho.* The principal *árcades mineiros* were Cláudio Manoel da Costa (1729-1789), Tomás Antônio Gonzaga (1744-1810?), and Manuel Inácio da Silva Alvarenga (1749-1814). Having come of age in the atmosphere of the Portuguese Enlightenment in Coimbra, they developed in the colony, and specifically in the then extremely wealthy town of Vila Rica, a coherently neoclassical literature in which bucolic and idyllic motifs, taken from classical tradition and filtered through a Renaissance or Petrarchan sensibility, are incorporated into the local landscape. There is a certain tendency in the interpretation of Brazilian literary history to consider the *árcades* poets as anticipating a local, nativist, and properly Brazilian spirit—an interpretation that is reinforced by their involvement in the failed movement for local autonomy that became known as the Inconfidência Mineira (1789). This idea of a "Brazilian" tone in the neoclassical literature that flourished in Minas Gerais would evidently merit a discussion longer than is possible here.

[19] *Quilombolas* were the residents of *quilombos* (see note 8).

[20] Bosi refers here to the encomiastic literature that flourished, beginning in the eighteenth century, in the context of colonial high society and around the Academies, which brought together men of letters and members of the local elite. This literary production generally consisted of poetry of quite poor quality and is often valorized in the context of Brazilian literary history as the precursor to the more coherent production of the *árcades mineiros.* In his own history of Brazilian literature, Bosi suggests that the Academies were "the last center of Baroque literature [in Brazil] and the first signal of a living humanistic culture in our society that existed outside the convents." For this reason, "their contributions to history and to learning in general may have been more relevant than the heavy Gongoric legacy of its versifiers" (*História concisa* 48).

[21] This is a reference to the Dutch occupation of the Pernambuco region of northeastern Brazil, which occurred during the first half of the seventeenth century and in the context of the Dutch West India Company's military and commercial expansion. Between 1637 and 1643, Recife (the capital of Pernambuco) was governed by Maurice of Nassau. During this period, which was one of considerable urban development, artists like Frans Post and Albert Eckhout were active in Brazil.

22 The period of Brazil's Second Reign (1840-1889) in a way gave form to an entire political and literary tradition that would remain alive and active for many years, even in the more modern instances, in which Romanticism was rejected or repressed from an aesthetic point of view. What must be kept in mind is that during the nineteenth century, literature, the visual arts, and historiography searched hand in hand for the nation's founding myths. In terms of literary production, the affirmation of local feeling was coupled with the investigation of a desired collective identity. The best known of the first wave of Romantics are the poet Domingos José Gonçalves de Magalhães (1811-1882), the painter and poet Manuel de Araújo Porto Alegre (1808-1879), and the chronicler and historian Francisco Adolfo de Varnhagen (1816-1878).

23 The Aviz (or Avis) dynasty began in 1385 with Dom João I and continued until 1580, when Portugal came under Spanish dominion, where it would remain until 1640. The first edition of Camões's *Os Lusíadas* (1572) was published a few short years before the disappearance of the King D. Sebastião in the legendary battle of Alcácer-Quibir in 1578. This disappearance would give rise to the long-lasting myth of *sebastianismo,* of considerable importance for Portuguese history and literature.

24 Francisco de Sá de Miranda (1481-1558) is one of the authors of the *Cancioneiro Geral,* a volume compiled by Garcia de Resende at the beginning of the sixteenth century, which contains a vast amount of courtly poetry written in Spanish and Portuguese. As a writer, Sá de Miranda falls between traditional Iberian rhetoric and the classicizing tendencies of Italy, which he familiarized himself with during his travels in the homeland of the Renaissance. In his poetry he idealizes traditional noble values in depicting the feverish national pursuit of commercial and imperial expansion with skepticism and disdain.

25 This old saying, the Portuguese version of "Navigare necesse est, vivere non est necesse" ("Navegar é preciso, viver não é preciso" [It is necessary to sail, it is not necessary to live]), was immortalized in the language of Camões by the Portuguese modernist poet Fernando Pessoa, who associated it with an inescapable and imperious need for poetic creation, understood by him as part of a mystical Portuguese soul.

26 Jean de Léry and Hans Staden are among the most important chroniclers of the period, falling during the mid-sixteenth century, in which the coastal area between São Vicente and Rio de Janeiro was the site of conflicts between the Portuguese and French, who had established a Calvinist colony in Rio de Janeiro, bringing the European religious wars to the New World. The testimony of Staden, a German who was held captive by the Tupinambás, provides one of the most famous accounts of cannibalism in the New World. The work of the Portuguese Fernão Cardim, who spent many years in Brazil and occupied important positions there as a member of the Company of Jesus, dates from the final decades of the sixteenth century.

[27] In his *História concisa da literatura brasileira,* Bosi describes the *Peregrino da América* by the Bahian Nuno Marques Pereira (1652-1728) as a "long allegory in dialog form, very close in style to the Spanish and Portuguese moralists who simplify the ascetic principles of the Counter-Reformation. [...] As in the pages of Father Manuel Bernardes, though with less grace and fluidity, *Peregrino da América* resurrects an entire body of medieval symbolism relative to which the Iberian Baroque appears at times merely as a cheap copy" (46-7).

[28] The term *caipira* may simply refer to a person who lives outside Brazil's urban centers. More specifically, it designates the inhabitants (or that which relates to them) of the rural areas of southeastern Brazil, and particularly of the interior of the state of São Paulo. The term was originally reserved for itinerant peasants or the sort of person the critic Antonio Candido called an "atrophied *bandeirante.*" Depending on context, *caipira* may have a pejorative charge, signifying something or someone that is unsophisticated or crude.

[29] This is a reference to the importance of the "Pastorais" and to the politicization of the Catholic clergy during the years of the dictatorship, due principally to the influx of Liberation Theology. During the period described by Bosi in this passage, the Catholic political and religious imagination was still strongly marked by the intellectual opening brought about by the Second Vatican Council in the first half of the 1960s.

[30] Beginning in 1889, the first years of the Republic in Brazil witnessed the appearance of movements of social resistance and revolt, particularly in rural areas, which quickly took on a religious and monarchist character. Charismatic leaders and mystics advanced an eschatological discourse that, to the ears of the young republican government, registered as the most regressive and dangerous of threats. Canudos was an enormous popular settlement founded in the backlands of Bahia during the final decade of the nineteenth century by a group led by Antônio Conselheiro. The so-called "Canudos war" gained fame not only for its violence and for the massacres committed by the government forces in their various attempts to take the town, but also because (as Bosi mentions in his endnote) Euclides da Cunha immortalized the affair in *Os Sertões,* one of the masterpieces of Brazilian literature (translated into English by Samuel Putnam as *Rebellion in the Backlands*). The Contestado war occurred during the first decade of the twentieth century, in the interior of the state of Santa Catarina, and involved peasants inspired by a monk named José Maria. In this case, the conflict's character as a struggle for land is clearer than it was in the case of Canudos, but the Contestado affair did not attract a literary chronicler of the stature of Euclides da Cunha.

[31] Graciliano Ramos (1892-1953) is perhaps the most engaged of the writers who flourished in the wake of Brazilian modernism (whose "heroic period" occurred during the 1920s). For Bosi, he represents "the highest point in the tension between the I of the writer and the society that forms him," and is characterized by a "realism [that is] neither organic nor spontaneous, [but] critical" (*História concisa* 400-402). *Vidas secas* (1938), the best known of Ramos's novels, narrates

the desperate flight of a family of *retirantes* from a drought plaguing the Brazilian northeast, which in the novel also becomes an existential journey.

32 Aside from being, respectively, a Parnassian poet and an important literary critic, Amadeu Amaral (1875-1929) and Sílvio Romero (1851-1914) made fundamental contributions to the study of the folkloric traditions of the Brazilian interior. The writings of these and other folklorists would form the basis for the modernist poet Mário de Andrade's later studies of popular culture and investigations in ethnomusicology, which he undertook principally in the 1930s and 40s.

33 *Leixa-pren* is a typical feature of the Galician-Portuguese *cantigas,* which are among the earliest texts in the Portuguese language. The term refers to the repetition of poetic verses in successive stanzas, through a process that consists of "taking up" (*pren*) what has been "left behind" (*leixa*).

34 The architect Luís Saia (1911-1975), a scholar of Brazil's historical patrimony, was the head of the famous "Folkloric Research Mission" that Mário de Andrade, then the director of the city of São Paulo's Cultural Secretariat, sent to the Brazilian north and northeast in 1938 with the purpose of documenting, through audio and film recordings, photographs, interviews, and fieldwork, evidence of popular music in order to "show Brazil to the Brazilians," as Saia himself expressed it at the time. The material recorded by the mission was recently collected in a CD box set (*Mário de Andrade—Missão de Pesquisas Folclóricas*) and is also partially available through the U.S. Library of Congress's "Endangered Music Project," on a CD entitled *The Discoteca Collection—Missão de Pesquisas Folclóricas* (Rykodisc, 1997).

35 According to Mário de Andrade, the *cheganças de mouros,* or "arrivals of the Moors" (an expression coined by Sílvio Romero), fall within the body of Brazilian dramatic dances. *Cheganças,* featuring the reenactment of the wars between the Christians and the Moors, refer back to ancient Iberian reenactments that were performed even before the fall of Granada in 1492. Again according to Andrade, *congos* were Afro-Brazilian dramatic dances that reenacted a king's coronation, or an "embassy" to the king. These traditions interact with each other, and their presence may be detected in more recent manifestations of northeastern folklore, such as the *maracatus* of Recife. For more on this subject, see Andrade's *Danças dramáticas do Brasil.*

36 Giuseppe Ungaretti (1888-1970), one of the most important names in twentieth-century Italian literature, spent time in Brazil and taught at the University of São Paulo between 1936 and 1942. The trip referred to here took place a long time after this period, on one of his return voyages to Brazil. On this occasion, Bosi himself put Ungaretti in contact with his brother-in-law, the engineer and amateur photographer Sérgio Antônio de Pádua Frederico (1939-1985), who accompanied Ungaretti on a trip to discover the *barroco mineiro.* The photographs relating to this trip have unfortunately been lost.

37 The French Artistic Mission arrived in Brazil in 1816, with the Portuguese court already having been installed in Rio de Janeiro from 1808. This relocation of

the metropolitan government to one of its colonies in the context of the Napoleonic wars then affecting Europe was in and of itself a unique historical phenomenon. In 1816, D. João VI founded the Escola Real das Ciências, Artes e Ofícios (Royal School for the Sciences, Arts, and Professions) in Rio de Janeiro, which would count Jean-Baptiste Debret, Nicolas-Antoine Taunay, and Auguste-Henri-Victor Montigny among its instructors. The neoclassical values they brought with them from France entered into conflict with the Baroque tradition, which a century later the modernist movement would recuperate and valorize in its own way. The idea of travel is of fundamental importance in understanding the modernist movement's "rediscovery" of Brazil. It is nonetheless ironic that the modernists' mythical journey to Minas Gerais, which they made in order to discover Brazil's true past, was immortalized by the presence of the Swiss poet Blaise Cendrars, who accompanied the entire modernist troop in being marveled by the *barroco mineiro* during the Holy Week of 1924.

38 The Regency period began in 1831 when D. Pedro I, the son of D. João VI, returned to Portugal and abdicated the Brazilian throne, which he had occupied since 1822, in favor of his son who was then a young child. The son, D. Pedro II, was only crowned in 1840, thereby beginning the Second Reign, which would last until 1889, the year in which a Republic was proclaimed in Brazil.

39 The title of "regretful Romantic" was given to Gonçalves de Magalhães (see note 22 above regarding Magalhães and Araújo Porto Alegre) by the modernist writer Alcântara Machado. The painter Jean-Baptiste Debret (1768-1848), a member of the French Artistic Mission, produced an extremely rich archive of images that document the customs of Rio de Janeiro. Debret's works, which depict social contrasts visible in the landscape of Brazilian society and feature a sizable gallery of subjects from various classes and backgrounds, nearly always show a sharp "ethnographic" sense, as we would call it today. Along with the paintings of Johann Moritz Rugendas, Debret's work is one of the most important iconographic resources available for the study of Brazil during the first half of the nineteenth century. The artist's spirit of exploration in depicting a rich tropical imagery, along with his sometimes grandiose and dramatic projections of local scenery, influenced decisively the first Brazilian Romantic writers and set the foundations for the nineteenth-century nationalist and Romantic school of Brazilian painting.

40 Bernardo Guimarães (1825-1884) is one of a series of regionalist writers who, following the trail blazed by José de Alencar, dedicated himself to a minute (and generally cliché-ridden) description of the land and people of the Brazilian interior. His novels, which include *O seminarista* (it is from this text that Bosi takes the passage on Aleijadinho) and *A escrava Isaura,* are simultaneously "sertanejas" (that is, of or relating to the *sertão,* backlands) and "semi-populares," according to Bosi's own classification (*História concisa* 144).

Works Cited

Amaral, Amadeu. *Tradições populares*. São Paulo: Hucitec, 1976.

Andrade, Mário de. *Aspectos das artes plásticas no Brasil*. Belo Horizonte: Itatiaia, 1984.

———. *Danças dramáticas do Brasil*. Ed. Oneyda Alvarenga. Belo Horizonte: Itatiaia, 2002.

Anchieta, José de. *Cartas, informações, fragmentos históricos e sermões (1554-94)*. Rio de Janeiro: Academia Brasileira de Letras, 1933.

Azevedo, Thales de. *Igreja e Estado em tensão e crise*. São Paulo: Ática, 1978.

Bhabha, Homi. *Nation and Narration*. London: Routledge, 1990.

Bosi, Alfredo. *Dialética da colonização*. São Paulo: Companhia das Letras, 1992.

———. *História concisa da literatura brasileira*. São Paulo: Cultrix, 1994.

———. *Literatura e resistência*. São Paulo: Companhia das Letras, 2002.

———. *O ser e o tempo da poesia*. São Paulo: Cultrix, 1993.

———. "Sobre alguns modos de ler poesia: memórias e reflexões." *Leitura de poesia*. São Paulo: Ática, 2001. 7-48.

Burckhardt, Jacob. *Force and Freedom: Reflections on History*. Ed. James Hasting Nichols. New York: Pantheon Books, 1943.

Camões, Luís Vaz de. *The Lusíads*. Trans. Landeg White. Oxford: Oxford UP, 1997.

Césaire, Aimé. *Discours sur le colonialisme*. Paris: Présence Africaine, 1955.

Childe, Gordon. *Man Makes Himself*. London: Watts, 1965.

Cidade, Hernâni. *A literatura portuguesa e a expansão ultramarina*. Coimbra: A. Amado, 1963-64.

Cunha, Euclides da. *Os Sertões: Campanha de Canudos*. Ed. Leopoldo M. Bernucci. São Paulo: Ateliê Editorial, 2001.

Dupront, Alphonse. *L'acculturazione. Per un nuovo rapporto tra ricerca storica e scienze umane*. Turin: Einaudi, 1971.

Durán Luzio, Juan. "Bartolomé de las Casas y Michel de Montaigne: escritura y lectura del Nuevo Mundo." *Revista Chilena de Literatura* 37 (1991): 7-24.

Eliot, T.S. *Notes Toward the Definition of Culture*. New York: Harcourt, Brace and Company, 1949.

Etzel, Eduardo. *Imagens religiosas de São Paulo*. São Paulo: Melhoramentos, 1971.

Faoro, Raymundo. *Os donos do poder: Formação do patronato político brasileiro*. Porto Alegre: Globo, 1958.

Flores, Juan. *From Bomba to Hip-Hop: Puerto Rican Culture and Latino Identity*. New York: Columbia UP, 2000.

Forcellini, Aegidio. *Lexicon totius latinitatis*. Padua: Typis Seminarii, 1940.

Franco, Maria Sylvia Carvalho. "Organização social do trabalho no período colonial." Paulo Sérgio Pinheiro, ed., *Trabalho escravo, economia e sociedade*. Rio de Janeiro: Paz e Terra, 1984. 143-192.

Freyre, Gilberto. *The Mansions and the Shanties: The Making of Modern Brazil*. New York: Alfred Knopf, 1963.

———. *The Masters and the Slaves: A Study in the Development of Brazilian Civilization*. New York: Alfred Knopf, 1946.

Furtado, Celso. *Formação econômica do Brasil*. Rio de Janeiro: Fundo de Cultura, 1959.

Galich, Manuel. *Nuestros primeros padres*. Havana: Casa de las Américas, 1979.

Gastaut, Henri. "Alguns comentários a respeito do culto do crânio." *A unidade do homem. Invariantes biológicos e universais culturais*. Org. Centro Royaumont para uma Ciência do Homem. Vol. 3. São Paulo: Cultrix/Edusp, 1978.

Godinho, Vitorino Magalhães. *Economia dos descobrimentos henriquinos*. Lisboa: Livraria Sá da Costa, 1962.

González y Perez, Rex. *Argentina indígena, vísperas de la conquista*. Buenos Aires: Editorial Paidós, 1972.

Gorender, Jacob. *O escravismo colonial*. São Paulo: Ática, 1977.

Gramsci, Antonio. *Il materialismo storico*. Roma: Editori Riuniti, 1975.

Gutiérrez, Gustavo. *Dios o el oro en las Indias. Siglo XVI*. Lima: Instituto Bartolomé de las Casas Rimac, 1989.

Hart, Mickey and Alan Jabbour, prod. *The Discoteca Collection—Missão de Pesquisas Folclóricas*. Rykodisc, 1997.

Holanda, Sérgio Buarque de. *Caminhos e fronteiras*. Rio de Janeiro: José Olympio, 1957.

———. *Raízes do Brasil*. Rio de Janeiro: José Olympio, 1956.

Hoornaert, Eduardo. "Rio de Janeiro, uma Igreja perseguida." *Revista Eclesiástica Brasileira* 31 (1971): 590-619.

Jaeger, Werner. *Paideia: The Ideals of Greek Culture*. Trans. Gilbert Highet. New York and Oxford: Oxford UP, 1939-44.

Lacombe, Américo Jacobina. "A Igreja no Brasil colonial." *História geral da civilização brasileira*. Dir. Sérgio Buarque de Holanda. Vol. 2. São Paulo: Difel, 1977.

Larousse du XXe Siècle. Dir. Paul Augé. Paris: Librairie Larousse, 1928.

Machado, Lourival Gomes. *Barroco mineiro*. São Paulo: Editora Perspectiva, 1978.

Magne, Augusto. *Dicionário Etimológico da Língua Latina*. Vol. 4. Rio de Janeiro: MEC, 1962.

Mário de Andrade—Missão de Pesquisas Folclóricas. São Paulo: Secretaria de Cultura da Cidade de São Paulo & Centro Cultural São Paulo, 2006.

Marrou, Henri-Irénée. *A History of Education in Antiquity.* Trans. George Lamb. New York: Sheed and Ward, 1956.

Marx, Karl. *Capital: A Critique of Political Economy.* Trans. Samuel Moore and Edward Aveling. Vols. 1 and 3. Chicago: Charles H. Kerr & Company, 1906.

———. *Critique of Hegel's Philosophy of Right.* Cambridge: Cambridge UP, 1970.

———. *Pre-Capitalist Economic Formations.* Trans. Jack Cohen. New York: International Publishers, 1980.

Mesquita Filho, Júlio de. *Ensaios sul-americanos.* São Paulo: Livraria Martins, 1946.

Meyer, Claus. *Passos da Paixão: o Aleijadinho.* Rio de Janeiro: Edições Alumbramento/Livro-arte Editora, 1989.

Montaigne, Michel de. *The Essays of Michel de Montaigne.* Trans. M.A. Screech. London: Allen Lane/The Penguin Press, 1991.

Monteiro, Duglas Teixeira. *Os errantes do novo século.* São Paulo: Duas Cidades, 1976.

Morse, Richard, ed. *The Bandeirantes: The Historical Role of the Brazilian Pathfinders.* New York: Alfred A. Knopf, 1965.

Nixon, Paul, trans. "Rudens, or The Rope." *Plautus.* Vol. 4. Cambridge, MA: Harvard University Press/Loeb Classical Library, 1932.

Novais, Fernando. *Portugal e Brasil na crise do antigo sistema colonial.* São Paulo: Hucitec, 1979.

Oliveira, Myriam Andrade Ribeiro de, Olinto Rodrigues dos Santos Filho, and Antonio Fernando Batista dos Santos. *O Aleijadinho e sua oficina: Catálogo das esculturas devocionais.* São Paulo: Editora Capivara, 2002.

Pereira, Nuno Marques. *Compêndio narrativo do Peregrino da América. Em que se tratam vários discursos espirituais, e morais, com muitas advertências e documentos contra os abusos que se acham introduzidos pela malícia diabólica no Estado do Brasil.* Rio de Janeiro: Academia Brasileira de Letras, 1939.

Prado, Caio Jr. *Formação do Brasil contemporâneo.* São Paulo: Livraria Martins Editora, 1942.

Queiroz, Maria Isaura Pereira de. *O messianismo no Brasil e no mundo.* São Paulo: Dominus, 1965.

Queiroz, Maurício Vinhas de. *Messianismo e conflito social.* São Paulo: Ática, 1977.

Ribeiro, João. *O folclore, XXVII.* Rio de Janeiro: n/p, 1919.

Rocha, João Cezar de Castro, ed. *The Author as Plagiarist: The Case of Machado de Assis. Portuguese Literary & Cultural Studies* 13/14 (2006).

Rodrigues, Nina. *Os africanos no Brasil.* São Paulo: Nacional, 1977.

Romero, Sílvio. *Folclore brasileiro. Cantos populares do Brasil.* Belo Horizonte/São Paulo: Itatiaia/Edusp, 1985.

Saia, Luís. *Escultura popular brasileira.* São Paulo: Gaveta, 1944.

Slater, Candace. *Stories on a String: The Brazilian "Literatura de Cordel."* Berkeley: University of California Press, 1982.

Sodré, Nelson Werneck. *Formação da sociedade brasileira.* Rio de Janeiro: José Olympio, 1944.

Taunay, Afonso. *A missão artística de 1816.* Rio de Janeiro: MEC, 1956.

Verger, Pierre. *Notícias da Bahia — 1850.* Salvador: Corrupio, 1985.

Vico, Giambattista. *The New Science.* Trans. Thomas Goddard Bergin and Max Harold Fisch. Ithaca: Cornell UP, 1984.

Xidieh, Oswaldo Elias. "Cultura popular." *Feira Nacional da Cultura Popular.* São Paulo: Sesc, 1976.

———. *Narrativas pias populares.* São Paulo: Instituto de Estudos Brasileiros, 1967.

———. *Semana santa cabocla.* São Paulo: Instituto de Estudos Brasileiros, 1972.

Index

113

Photo Credits

Page 86

Meyer, Claus. *Passos da Paixão: o Aleijadinho.* Rio de Janeiro: Edições Alumbramento/Livro-arte Editora, 1989. 99.

Page 87

Oliveira, Myriam Andrade Ribeiro de, Olinto Rodrigues dos Santos Filho, and Antonio Fernando Batista dos Santos. *O Aleijadinho e sua oficina: Catálogo das esculturas devocionais.* São Paulo: Editora Capivara, 2002. 181.